STARTERS & SIDES
MADE Easy

FOOD STYLIST — AMIT FARBER
PHOTOGRAPHY — DANIEL LAILAH

DESIGN — RACHELADLERDESIGN.COM
PUBLISHER — ARTSCROLL / SHAAR PRESS

Leah Schapira & Victoria Dwek

Published by **ARTSCROLL / SHAAR PRESS**
4401 Second Avenue / Brooklyn, NY 11232 / (718) 921-9000
www.artscroll.com

Distributed in Israel by **SIFRIATI / A. GITLER**
6 Hayarkon Street / Bnei Brak 51127 / Israel

Distributed in Europe by **LEHMANNS**
Unit E, Viking Business Park, Rolling Mill Road
Jarrow, Tyne and Wear, NE32 3DP / England

Distributed in Australia and New Zealand by **GOLDS WORLD OF JUDAICA**
3-13 William Street / Balaclava, Melbourne 3183, Victoria / Australia

Distributed in South Africa by **KOLLEL BOOKSHOP**
Ivy Common / 105 William Road / Norwood 2192 / Johannesburg, South Africa

ISBN-10: 1-4226-1422-0 / ISBN-13: 978-1-4226-1422-8
Printed in Canada by **NOBLE BOOK PRESS**

ACKNOWLEDGMENTS

WE ALWAYS SAY THAT OUR IDEAS AREN'T OURS.

We can be totally stumped, but then **Hashem** inserts something brilliant into our heads. We owe Him credit for every little teaspoon in this book.

Thank you to our chief taste-testers, our **husbands** and **children**, our encouraging parents, and the rest of our family. You helped cook, taste, babysit, and give valuable feedback. Thanks especially for your patience during the weeks of photo shoots. We hope you were buttered up by the buffet selection of starters and side dishes each night.

After the recipes were completed and tested, it takes the brilliance of our creative team to turn them into the book you see: our stylist, **Amit Farber**; our photographer, **Daniel Lailah**; our graphic artist **Rachel Adler**; and our operations manager, **Zalman Roth**.

Thank you to **Rechy Frankfurter** of *Ami Magazine* for pushing us to strive for better than best.

We have very talented and stylish friends and colleagues who helped us shop and select (and borrow!) the props used throughout this book. Thank you, **Shavy Weiss** and **Renee Muller**. It's always fun when you're around!

The **ArtScroll** team's dedication and enthusiasm are invigorating. Thanks to **Gedaliah Zlotowitz**, editor **Felice Eisner**, and designer **Devorah Bloch**, as well as **Judi Dick**, **Tova Ovits**, and the rest of the staff who kept things moving.

Thank You!

Leah and Victoria

Thanks to the cookkosher members who keep on stimulating us with their ideas.

Whenever we were inspired by a cookkosher member's contribution, you'll find the member's name on the recipe page. In appreciation, they'll each be receiving a copy of this cookbook.

We hope you enjoy these delicious, tried and true recipes, and that they stimulate you to have fun creating delicious meals for your families. And we hope we've made it easy, too.

ON THE COVER:

In the white bowl: **GEMELLI SALAD**, page 100.

In the glass bowls: **COUSCOUS AND CRUMBS**, page 56 and **CRISPY CHICKEN ROLLS**, page 84.

White bowl, tray, tablecloths, and cutlery available at Set Your Table in Lakewood, NJ and Monsey, NY. Glass bowls available at CB2.

For additional sources for items used throughout this book, see page 126.

INTRODUCTION

VICTORIA: *After Passover Made Easy* was done, it was time to think about what we'd write about next in our Made Easy series.

LEAH: I wanted to write a book describing all the different recipes we could make using pizza dough.

VICTORIA: And I told you that there's no way I'm willing to live on pizza dough for the next few months.

LEAH: I'll have to work on convincing you. But one thing was a must: If it wasn't going to be a book about pizza dough, it still had to feature the type of food that *we* love to cook and eat. So, we asked ourselves, "What kind of recipes do we need? What do our friends always ask us for?"

VICTORIA: And after polling all our neighbors … we concluded that we are always looking for more starter and side dish ideas.

LEAH: When I'm looking for a side dish on a weeknight, I'd like it to take minimal time to pull together, like the Zucchini and Scallion Fries on page 34 or the Golden Cauliflower on page 38. Even Sticky Red Potatoes (page 42) would be easy if I didn't always have to make a second batch.

VICTORIA: I agree. Dishes that are best fresh must be simple. When I'm entertaining, though, I don't want my kitchen to be messy when my guests arrive. I like to prepare in advance. I want to pull everything out of the freezer and pop it in the oven. That makes my life easy.

LEAH: True. Sometimes *easy* doesn't always mean *quick*. It's about having ideas that you love at your fingertips or using ingredients that you can find at your local supermarket. Of course, it always makes our lives easier when we know it's food our family will love!

VICTORIA: For no-stress food preparation, we added "Ahead" tips on every recipe in this book. If a recipe wasn't fridge- or freezer-friendly, it had to be fast. And even if you love your time-tested sides like roasted veggies, we give you easy ideas for expanding that repertoire in "Building Blocks" beginning on page 10.

LEAH: Since it also takes work to decide how you'll present your starters, we showed you great ideas that make pretty presentation easy. Look for "Plate It!" at the beginning of each section.

If you were invited to a meal at my house, one or two starters would already be plated on every dish. It could be a chicken skewer with a salad, like our Silan Chicken Salad (page 86) or a fish dish, like our Salmon with a Pocket (page 94).

VICTORIA: At my house, there are no premade plates or portions. All my starters (or as I call them, "mazzah," which means "small bites") would be in platters in the middle of the table. Take as many Falafel Cigars (page 76) as you like. Then ... bam ... all my mains and sides come out of the kitchen quickly, each in a large serving dish.

LEAH: My side dishes go where they belong. Plated on the side of the main.

VICTORIA: What if you don't even want a main?

LEAH: You might not if these are the starters and sides on the menu.

VICTORIA: I'm starting to feel sorry for those main dishes.

LEAH: No need! You can always "Make It a Main." Look for those ideas on page 126.

FLAVOR MADE EASY: A SPICE GUIDE

PEPPERCORNS

Pepper adds spiciness without changing the flavor of your food. That's why it's the most common spice in the world and works in almost every dish.

1 If you're freshly grinding your black pepper (recommended!), your spice jar will be filled with **WHOLE PEPPERCORNS**.

2 **FINE BLACK PEPPER**

3 We use **COARSE BLACK PEPPER** instead of fine black pepper throughout this book. The large flakes give food a pretty speckle without overpowering the flavor. White pepper is made from the intensely spicy seeds inside the black peppercorns.

GARLIC & ONION

Fresh garlic and onion are the kitchen go-to's for flavoring food, after salt and pepper. The dried versions are more convenient and very versatile.

4 **MINCED ONION** and garlic work great when you need texture along with flavor. Minced onion helps create a crust on Seared Pepper Tuna on page 100.

5 **ONION POWDER** adds a very subtle onion flavor, especially when it's used to enhance a dish that also includes fresh onion, as in our Spinach Spring Rolls on page 68.

6 We use **GARLIC POWDER** for a milder garlic flavor, but sometimes it's more practical than fresh garlic when flavor needs to be very evenly distributed, as in spice rubs on meat, or when spicing up our Flatbreads on page 18.

SALTS
What kind of salt should you use?

7 We used **KOSHER SALT** as our main cooking salt throughout this book.

8 **SEA SALT** is a finishing salt and will lose flavor during high temperature cooking. We sprinkled coarse sea salt on top of our Foccacia on page 48. You can use fine sea salt in place of table salt.

9 **TABLE SALT** belongs … on the table. If you use it for cooking, you'll need only ⅓ of the amount, or 1 teaspoon for every 1 tablespoon of kosher salt.

10 **CITRIC ACID**, also known as sour salt, can be used in place of lemon juice. Citric acid is used in sour candy.

EARTHY TONES

11 Leah says cu-min and Victoria says que-moon. But we both love **CUMIN** for its earthy flavor. Use it as a spice rub for meat, in salad dressing, on any roasted veggies, or in our modern version of couscous on page 56.

12 **MUSTARD POWDER** is made from dried mustard seeds, and its flavor is much more intense than prepared

CHILI PEPPERS
These red spices are made from dried chili peppers of varying intensity.

14 **CRUSHED RED PEPPER** is made from coarsely ground red chili peppers, with the addition of the seeds to intensify the heat. You'll usually need only a pinch.

15 **PAPRIKA**, commonly used in Hungarian cuisine, adds red color and a sweet smokiness to dishes. Paprika is at its best when it's heated with oil and is made from dried red bell peppers or mild chili peppers.

16 We use lots of **CHILI POWDER** throughout this book for a mild heat. Chili powder is actually a spice blend. Though the main ingredient is chili pepper, it also includes cumin, oregano, garlic, and salt for complete flavor.

17 .**CAYENNE PEPPER**, made from dried red chili peppers, will deliver the heat.

mustard. Use it as a base if you want to create your own flavor of mustard.

13 **TURMERIC** is part of the ginger family but its flavor is much more subtle. It's mainly used for its golden color and beauty, as in our Yemenite "Yellow" Orzo Rice on page 60.

HERBS

Although fresh herbs usually taste best, they're not always convenient. We specified when we used fresh or dried. You can use the frozen herb cubes in any of the recipes calling for fresh herbs throughout this book.

1 frozen cube = **1** teaspoon fresh herbs

3 frozen cubes = **1** tablespoon fresh herbs = **1** teaspoon dried herbs

1 **OREGANO** is also known as pizza spice and pairs well in similar dishes, as in our Tomato Tart on page 110.

2 Pretty **DILL** isn't just about cucumbers and pickles. Try it in mustard, mayo, and yogurt-based dips and dressings. It enhances the Asparagus and Kohlrabi Sippers on page 20.

3 It's about time you use **THYME**. The popular herb is common in French, Italian, and Mediterranean cooking and pairs well with butternut squash in comforting, savory recipes, such as our Winter Squash Ravioli on page 50.

4 **CILANTRO** is the "love it or hate it" herb with a refreshing flavor. Love it? Try it on our Golden Cauliflower on page 38.

5 **BAY LEAVES** give a woodsy and warm undertone to a dish. Remove before serving.

6 Refreshing fresh **MINT** is often used in fruity desserts, but the dried herb brightens up and perfectly complements peas, as in the Spring Pea Phyllo Purses on page 28.

7 Strongly scented, flowery **ROSEMARY** pairs well with poultry, lamb, meat, and potatoes. It turns olives into gourmet antipasti in the Rosemary Baked Olives on page 22.

8 **MAJORAM** is a close cousin to oregano.

9 **BASIL** deserves its popularity because of its versatility. It's not just for Italian dishes — it's every veggie's best friend. Our Green Beans on page 36 really love lots of it.

10 **PARSLEY** has a mild bitterness that helps to balance the flavors in savory dishes, as in our Barbecue Noodles on page 52.

SWEET OR SAVORY

These spices are most commonly found in sweet dishes, but can be used in savory recipes as well. When mixed together into a blend, they're often labeled as "Pumpkin Pie Spice" or "Apple Pie Spice."

11 Though **CINNAMON**, in sticks or ground, can be used in savory dishes, it's the star of the sweet plate. A little bit transforms our streusel on the Peach Cracker Crumble on page 120.

12 **ALLSPICE** gives a flowery, fragrant smell and taste to the Lehme B'agine on page 74 and as part of a spice blend in our Shwarma Egg Rolls on page 82. In the US, it also makes its way into sweet desserts when paired with cinnamon.

13 A teensy bit of **NUTMEG** pairs with cinnamon on top of a latte. Mace is a milder alternative.

14 Dried **GINGER** is the spice that gives gingerbread cookies their flavor. When substituting dried ginger for fresh in Asian dishes, use just a pinch as it's much more intense.

SPICE BLENDS

Some of our favorite spices are blends, where complementary flavors are pre-combined.

15 **PICKLING SPICE** is used for brining meats. We add some extra to the water when boiling corned beef.

16 All your favorite herbs blend together in **ITALIAN SEASONING** mix. It's perfect in tomato-based dishes or in any recipe using basil or oregano.

17 **STEAK SEASONING** is a mixture of various salts, peppers, and other spices. It enhances the appearance of the dish and offers meat and fish dishes loads of easy flavor.

18 Pull the ready-to-go **SHWARMA SPICE** out of your spice cabinet when you're grilling chicken or meat.

19 **ZA'ATAR** is a Middle-Eastern blend, usually made of sumac, sesame seeds, and oregano or thyme. It creates a lemony, herby, and rich seasoning that can even give new life to bread, veggies, or chummus.

BUILDING BLOCKS Mashed

VICTORIA: When I make the Winter Squash Ravioli (page 50), sometimes I want to steal some of the butternut squash filling and enjoy a bowl of the light, comforting, and naturally sweet mash on its own.

LEAH: I use broccoli or cauliflower to make a light mash. Sauté 1 onion and 2 pounds of thawed frozen broccoli. Add ¾ cup chicken stock, cover, and cook until broccoli is falling apart, about 15-25 minutes. Let cool, blend in a food processor, and season with salt and pepper.

1 What kind of potatoes make the best mash? It's okay to sacrifice some starchiness for flavor. If you love the taste of Yukon Golds, use them! You don't need to buy a sack of starchy Russets.

2 Mashed sweet potatoes tend to be stringy. Press them through a wire strainer or sieve for a mash that's smooth and sweet. For every three sweet potatoes, add one regular potato to the mixture to help create a creamier consistency.

3 Add foolproof flavor to your mash. Sauté crushed garlic or caramelize onions in oil and mix them into any type of mash.

4 You don't need to peel your potatoes. Make "smashed" potatoes instead. Use red potatoes and mash them with the skin on. Add in a couple of tablespoons mayonnaise and chopped scallions and season to taste.

5 Use butter instead of oil, and milk instead of cooking liquid for potatoes that are dreamy and dairy.

Green Mashed Potatoes

YIELD 2½ cups

INGREDIENTS

¼ *cup* packed fresh herbs (such as parsley, basil, or cilantro)

¼ *cup* oil

2 *lbs* peeled potatoes, cut into chunks

• salt and pepper to taste

INSTRUCTIONS

1. Soak herbs in boiling water for 3-4 minutes, to intensify the color and flavor while softening them, making them easier to blend into a smooth paste. (Boiling is unnecessary if using frozen herb cubes.)

2. Drain fresh herbs and combine with oil. Blend using an immersion blender or food processor.

3. Add potatoes to a large pot. Cover with water and bring to a boil over high heat. Reduce heat, cover, and simmer until potatoes are tender, 15-20 minutes. Drain. Reserve some of the cooking liquid.

4. In a large bowl, mash the potatoes using a potato masher. Add in herb oil. Mash until fully combined. Add in some of the reserved cooking liquid if needed to reach desired consistency.

5. Season with salt and pepper.

Roasted Veggies

LEAH: Whenever I serve roasted veggies on Friday night, the leftovers go into my salad the next day. I mix the veggies with Romaine lettuce, strips of grilled chicken or schnitzel, and a mayo-based dressing.

1 For best results, spread vegetables out on a baking sheet (don't crowd them in a baking pan) and roast at high temperature (higher...higher...400°F to 450°F is perfect).

2 It's not just about zucchini and peppers! Roast onions, sweet potatoes, tomatoes, eggplants, and carrots (halve 'em down the center). For quickie roasted veggies: asparagus and string beans are done in just 10 minutes.

3 What about flavor? You don't need much. Just a pinch of this and that. Here are some winning equations:

olive oil + basil + salt + pepper + pinch sugar

oil + soy sauce + garlic

olive oil + balsamic vinegar + salt + pepper

olive oil + cumin + garlic + salt

4 Never open a can of beets again! Roast them fresh for a naturally sweet side. Add unpeeled beets and a bit of water and oil to a baking pan. Cover and roast for 1 hour and 30 minutes. The peel will slide right off. Slice and serve with a simple balsamic vinaigrette: 3 tablespoons balsamic vinegar, 2 tablespoons olive oil, ½ teaspoon salt, and a pinch of coarse black pepper.

Roasted Garlic

YIELD 1 garlic head

INGREDIENTS

1	garlic head
2 Tbsp	olive oil
•	pinch salt
•	pinch Italian Seasoning

INSTRUCTIONS

1. Preheat oven to 350°F.

2. Cut off the top of the head to expose the tops of the cloves. Place on a piece of aluminum foil, drizzle with olive oil, and sprinkle with salt and Italian seasoning.

3. Wrap garlic in the foil and bake for 1 hour. Let cool.

4. To serve, break off a clove and squeeze the roasted garlic onto a soft piece of challah or any fresh bread. If you don't want to serve the unpeeled garlic cloves at the table, squeeze out the roasted garlic and whisk with additional olive oil to serve as a completed dip or spread.

In a rush? Separate the unpeeled cloves from the head and proceed as directed. You'll lose a bit on presentation, but the cloves will roast in about half the time.

USING ROASTED GARLIC

When garlic is roasted, sweet and creamy pulp oozes out of each clove when you press on the skin. Use the garlic as a spread or whisk into salad dressings. For a dairy meal, whisk the roasted garlic with olive oil, seasoning, and Parmesan cheese and toss it with cooked pasta.

I'll Have Some Rice

VICTORIA: My favorite rice is crunchy rice. Simply leave plain white rice on the hottest part of the hotplate or "blech" for hours on Shabbat day until it's golden and crunchy. Enjoy with coleslaw.

1 What kind of rice should you choose? For an all-around popular rice, try Carolina brand. Like mushy rice? Choose short grain rice, such as sushi, jasmine, or a brand like Goya.

2 Don't want to stand over a stove? Try Newlywed Rice. Why the name? It's often the first rice a new cook learns to prepare. Combine 1 cup rice, 2½ cups water, ¼ cup oil, and ¼ cup onion soup mix. Cover and bake at 350°F for about 1 hour.

3 Make an easy, flavorful Garlic Rice. Sauté crushed garlic in oil. Add uncooked rice and toast for a couple of minutes. Add chicken stock (instead of water), bring to a boil, lower heat, cover, and simmer until liquid is absorbed.

4 Have leftover rice? Make Fried Rice. This fried rice isn't really fried, but it is the perfect way to wake up leftover rice. Scramble some eggs, then sauté onions and whatever other veggies you have in your produce drawer; set aside. Heat 2 tablespoons oil and 1 teaspoon of your favorite spice. Pack your leftover rice into the pan and let it cook for about 3 minutes without stirring. Stir in 2 teaspoons soy sauce and reserved eggs and veggies.

5 Micro-Rice. Yes, you can make rice in the microwave! Rinse your rice and place it into a microwave-safe container with a lid. Cover rice with 1 inch water. Cover loosely and microwave for 9-10 minutes. Let rice sit for 3 minutes before removing from microwave.

Perfect Rice

INSPIRED BY
COOKKOSHER MEMBER
vanillasugar

INGREDIENTS

1	cup rice
3 Tbsp	oil
1½ cups	water (or amount specified on package)
•	salt to taste

INSTRUCTIONS

1. Wash and drain the rice very well. This step removes the excess starch, which makes rice mushy.

2. Heat oil in a medium saucepan over medium heat. Add rice and toast for 1 minute. Season with salt. Add water and bring rice to a boil. Immediately cover and lower heat to the lowest possible setting. Let simmer until water has evaporated, about 15-20 minutes.

3. Remove rice from heat. Uncover pot and cover with a clean dishcloth. Place the pot cover on the cloth and let rice steam for 5 minutes (the dishcloth will absorb the excess moisture, resulting in fluffy rice).

OTHER RICE

Though we've used white rice in this recipe, you can use the same tips to prepare any type of rice perfectly. Simply adjust the amount of water and cooking time.

PLATE IT!

Make a bowl to hold your Teriyaki Mushrooms (page 26), just the way you enjoy them in the restaurant.

1 Start with 6-inch wheat tortillas or wraps. Bring a pot of oil to boil. Press the tortilla in between 2 ladles to form into a bowl. When oil is hot, slip the tortilla with the ladles into the oil.

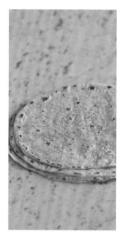

2 Fry until tortilla bowl is golden brown and drain on a paper towel-lined plate.

3 Fill bowl with mushrooms and top with cashews.

4 Finish your dish with chopped scallions or a scallion bundle, as shown in the photo. To create the bundle, slice the scallions into very thin strips.

5 Using one thin strip, tie a number of scallion strips together.

6 Top mushrooms with scallion bundle.

VEGETABLES

Flatbreads with Eggplant Salad

INGREDIENTS

FLATBREADS

- 8-10 egg roll wraps
- • salt
- • garlic powder
- • dried basil

EGGPLANT SALAD

- 1 large eggplant, cut into 1-inch cubes
- • salt for sprinkling
- 1 red pepper, cut into strips
- 3 Tbsp oil
- ¾ tsp salt
- • pinch coarse black pepper
- 3 Tbsp sweet chili sauce
- 2 tsp vinegar
- 2 scallions, sliced

INSTRUCTIONS

1. Preheat oven to 375°F. Line two baking sheets with parchment paper.

2. Cut each egg roll wrap into 5 strips or triangles (you can stack them and cut through a few at a time). Spread on prepared baking sheets. Spray strips with nonstick cooking spray and sprinkle with salt, garlic, and basil, about ½ teaspoon each, or to taste.

3. Bake until flatbreads are light golden brown, about 8 minutes. Set aside.

4. Prepare the eggplant salad: Sprinkle salt over eggplant cubes and let sit for 15 minutes. Rinse well and pat dry.

5. Raise oven temperature to 450°F. Spread eggplant and red pepper on a baking sheet. Toss vegetables with oil. Season with salt and pepper. Bake for 30 to 40 minutes, until eggplant is cooked through and pepper begins to blister.

6. Place eggplant and pepper into a bowl. While still warm, toss with sweet chili sauce, vinegar, and scallions. Serve with flatbreads at room temperature.

YIELD
6-8 servings

When salting eggplant, place a few cubes into a colander, add salt, then continue to add eggplant cubes with a sprinkling of salt. This way, they are all salted and ready to be washed.

If serving these flatbreads alongside chummus or techineh, swap out the basil for cumin, za'atar, or sumac.

THIS salad was the first recipe developed for this book. I love sweet chili sauce. It's my favorite condiment. But I always felt the salad was lonely.   –L

I was also searching for a salad to go with these super-easy flatbreads, which have always been a favorite in my house.   –V

So we made a shidduch. When I made these flatbreads to serve with the salad, my guests were very upset when they finished them all. On Shabbos afternoon, they asked, "Are you sure you don't have any more amazing flatbreads? How did you get them so thin and crispy?" They thought I had made them from scratch. Who's going to tell them?   –L

AHEAD: Both the flatbreads and the eggplant salad can be made up to a few days ahead. Store them in airtight containers, keeping the flatbreads at room temperature and the eggplant dip refrigerated.

Asparagus AND Kohlrabi Sippers

INGREDIENTS

1 Tbsp	oil
1	onion, chopped
1 lb	asparagus, trimmed
1	large kohlrabi, chopped (1-1¼ cups)
2 cups	chicken stock
1½ tsp	salt, or to taste
•	pinch coarse black pepper
3 Tbsp	chopped fresh dill

INSTRUCTIONS

1. Heat oil in a large saucepan over medium heat. Add onion and sauté until soft, about 7 minutes.

2. Add asparagus, kohlrabi, and chicken stock to the pot. Bring to a boil. Cover, lower heat to medium-low, and simmer for 25-30 minutes. The kohlrabi should be very tender.

3. Purée soup using an immersion blender (or transfer to a blender). Season with salt and pepper. Top with dill before serving.

You can also use green or white frozen or jarred asparagus.

YIELD
4-6 servings

Kohlrabi is a sweet and crisp member of the turnip family. It's also delicious raw. Its refreshing crunch makes it a good replacement for cucumbers, radishes, or cabbage in salads.

If you like your soup to be chunkier, reserve some finely diced asparagus. Add it into the pot after puréeing and simmer for 5 minutes before serving.

I would never have thought to combine asparagus and kohlrabi. That was my mother-in-law's idea. I'd always wondered why the majority of her soups included kohlrabi and assumed it was because she likes it so much. When she gave me this quick recipe, I finally asked, "Why kohlrabi?" She told me that she uses it to thicken soups instead of using a potato. That's what gives this soup its velvety, delectable texture. And of course, the flavor is great too.

–L.

AHEAD: This soup will freeze well. If the soup is very thick upon reheating, add additional water and season to taste.

Za'atar AND Rosemary Baked Olives

INGREDIENTS

ZA'ATAR BLACK OLIVES

2	(6-oz) cans whole black olives, drained
2 tsp	za'atar
4	garlic cloves, minced
2 Tbsp	olive oil

ROSEMARY GREEN OLIVES

12 oz	whole green olives, drained
1 tsp	dried rosemary
4	garlic cloves, minced
2 Tbsp	olive oil

INSTRUCTIONS

1. Preheat oven to 375°F.

2. Prepare the za'atar black olives: In a baking dish, combine olives, za'atar, garlic, and olive oil. Bake, uncovered, for 40 minutes.

3. Prepare the rosemary green olives: In a baking dish, combine olives, rosemary, garlic, and olive oil. Bake, uncovered, for 40 minutes. You can serve the olives separately, or combine them in one serving dish. These olives turn into a perfect spread for garlic bread or challah if you smash them up a bit.

Can't find za'atar? Make your own: Combine ¼ cup sumac, 1 tablespoon sesame seeds, 1 tablespoon thyme, 1 tablespoon oregano, and 1 teaspoon salt in a food processor or mini chopper and blend.

YIELD
about 4 cups

INSPIRED BY COOKKOSHER MEMBER
wchervony

TIDBIT:
Za'atar spice was originally made from the za'atar plant, also known as the aizov plant, which is native to Israel. Because it is a protected species in danger of becoming extinct, it can no longer be harvested freely. Today's za'atar spice blends are made from a variety of herbs instead.

To prepare the toasted bread disks as pictured, use a cookie cutter to cut a circle from a slice of bread. Brush with olive oil and bake until golden.

WHEN these olives bake, they shrink a bit and the flavor intensifies, so they're even more flavorful than any "raw" spiced olives. During an olive taste test, these two olive-and-spice combinations were our favorite. Pick one or prepare and serve them both.

I love that I can toss the ingredients together, throw them in the oven, and not do anything else. Serve them along with the salads and dips during the first course of your meal. Your guests will think you splurged on some gourmet antipasti.   –V

AHEAD: You can prepare these olives up to one week ahead. Keep refrigerated and serve at room temperature.

Coleslaw Balls with Jalapeño Dip

INGREDIENTS

16 oz	coleslaw mix
1½ tsp	salt
3	garlic cloves, minced
½ tsp	coarse black pepper
¼ cup	flour
3 Tbsp	cornstarch
•	oil, for frying

JALAPEÑO DIP

¾ cup	mayonnaise
2	scallions, chopped
1	jalapeño pepper, seeds and ribs removed, chopped
2 Tbsp	water
1 Tbsp	lemon juice
½ tsp	salt
•	pinch coarse black pepper
•	pinch sugar

INSTRUCTIONS

1. Place cabbage into a large colander. Sprinkle with salt and let sit 15 minutes. Using both hands, squeeze cabbage very well to remove the excess water (it won't look watery to the eye, but plenty of liquid will come out when you squeeze).

2. In a large bowl, combine cabbage, garlic, pepper, flour, and cornstarch. Mix until mixture becomes dough-like. Using a tablespoon and damp hands, form into falafel-sized balls.

3. Heat 2-3 inches oil in a saucepan over medium-high heat. Fry balls in hot oil until golden on all sides, 4-5 minutes total.

4. Prepare the jalapeño dip: In a small bowl, combine mayonnaise, scallions, jalapeño pepper, water, lemon juice, salt, pepper, and sugar. Using an immersion blender, blend until smooth. Serve alongside coleslaw balls.

YIELD
20-30 balls

Make your own coleslaw mix: Combine 16 ounces shredded green cabbage with 1 shredded carrot.

Whenever using jalapeño peppers, remember to wear gloves — and keep your hands away from your eyes.

VICTORIA is a coleslaw addict. She eats it with everything. The problem is that she thinks the shredded cabbage and carrot combo is best with mayonnaise in traditional deli-style. I think coleslaw mix was created to make it easy to serve great appetizers. I use coleslaw with some pastrami as a quick filling for egg rolls, and now I tear open a bag to make these amazing coleslaw balls. Don't let the name fool you — these balls have nothing in common with coleslaw. Think: Crispy falafel meets latke.

–L.

AHEAD: You can freeze these balls, even after they are already fried! To reheat, spread them on a baking sheet and heat, uncovered, in a preheated oven for about 10 minutes.

Teriyaki Mushrooms

INGREDIENTS

1 Tbsp	oil
1	small onion, thinly sliced
1	(10-oz) package baby bella mushrooms, large ones halved

TERIYAKI SAUCE

½ cup	sugar
¼ cup	rice vinegar
3 Tbsp	soy sauce
2	garlic cloves, crushed
2 tsp	cornstarch dissolved in 1 Tbsp water
2 Tbsp	cashews
1	scallion, chopped

INSTRUCTIONS

1. Heat oil in a sauté pan over high heat. Add onion and sauté for 3-4 minutes, stirring occasionally. Add mushrooms and sauté for 5 additional minutes.

2. Remove mushrooms and onions from the pan.

3. Prepare the sauce: Add sugar, rice vinegar, soy sauce, and garlic to the same pan. Stir to combine and bring to a boil. Stir in cornstarch mixture and cook until sauce has thickened, about 6-8 minutes.

4. Return mushrooms and onions to the pan and toss to combine. Toss with cashews and scallions before serving.

YIELD
4 servings

Serving a dairy meal? Dip cubes of halloumi cheese into beaten egg, flour, egg again, and breadcrumbs. Fry until golden. Serve some cheese cubes over the mushrooms.

Make this mushroom bowl just like the restaurants do by deep-frying a 6-inch round tortilla wrap (or 5-inch square egg roll wrapper). See Plate It! on page 16.

IT seems that every kosher restaurant ends up with a bunch of Asian dishes on the menu, even when they claim to be serving American, Italian, or Middle Eastern food. Perhaps it's because Jews love Asian dishes. Maybe it's that umami addictive flavor of soy that keeps us coming back. Versions of this dish have appeared on menus from Jerusalem to New Jersey, converting non-mushroom eaters to mushroom lovers. Now, you can make this crowd-pleaser at home. —L.

AHEAD: Like restaurant food, Teriyaki Mushrooms are best when made fresh. For easier preparation, you can mix the sauce ingredients together in advance.

Spring Pea Phyllo Purses

INGREDIENTS

¼ cup	water
1 Tbsp	oil
1 Tbsp	sugar
1	large leek, cut into rings
1	garlic clove, crushed
1½ cups	spring peas, fresh or frozen
¼ tsp	salt, or to taste
¼ tsp	dried mint
¼ tsp	dried basil
10	sheets phyllo dough

INSTRUCTIONS

1. In a large sauté pan over medium heat, combine water, oil, and sugar. Bring to a boil. Lower heat and add leeks and garlic. Cook, stirring occasionally, until water is absorbed and leeks are golden and caramelized, about 30 minutes. Stir in peas, salt, mint, and basil and cook for 1 minute. Remove from heat.

2. Stack 5 phyllo sheets and cut into 6 squares. Repeat with remaining 5 phyllo sheets for a total of 12 squares.

3. Preheat the oven to 400°F. Grease a muffin tin. Place one phyllo square over a muffin cup and press into the center. Spoon in 2 tablespoons of spring pea mixture. You can leave the purse open or pinch the wrapper together at the top to form a sack. Spray the top of the dough generously with nonstick cooking spray. Repeat with remaining squares. Bake until tops are beginning to turn golden at the edges, about 10 minutes.

YIELD
12 purses

You can defrost the phyllo dough in the refrigerator and take it out when you're ready to work. Don't leave it uncovered on the counter for long or it will dry out.

Phyllo is also spelled fillo or filo.

THERE are certain vegetables that I look out for when the season arrives. One of those is fresh spring peas. When peas are picked, the sugars begin turning into starches right away. That's why fresh peas taste so different from frozen. But no matter the season, you can serve these peas in their delicate phyllo shells for a pretty appetizer, or on their own for an easy, bright, and refreshing side dish.   –V.

AHEAD: Freeze these purses before baking. Thaw and bake when ready to serve.

Broccoli-Stuffed Artichokes

INGREDIENTS

3 Tbsp	olive oil, divided
2	large shallots, finely diced
1	(24-oz) bag broccoli florets, thawed, halved
2	garlic cloves, crushed
½ cup	white wine, divided
1½ tsp	salt
½ cup	panko crumbs, divided
•	zest and juice of 1 lemon
½ tsp	dried basil
2	eggs, beaten
16	artichoke bottoms (from 2 [14-oz] bags frozen artichoke bottoms, thawed, or 4 [15-oz] cans artichoke bottoms)

INSTRUCTIONS

1. Heat 1 tablespoon olive oil in a sauté pan over medium-low heat. Add shallots and sauté for 3 minutes. Add broccoli and garlic. Pour in ¼ cup white wine and season with salt. Cook until broccoli is tender but still bright green, about 15 minutes. Stir in ¼ cup panko, lemon zest, and basil. Remove from heat. Stir in eggs.

2. Stuff broccoli mixture into the cavity of each artichoke bottom. Place into a 9 x 13-inch baking pan. Sprinkle with remaining panko crumbs.

3. Pour lemon juice, remaining 2 tablespoons olive oil, and remaining ¼ cup white wine into the bottom of the pan (this liquid will flavor the artichokes). Bake, uncovered, for 25 minutes. To brown the panko crumbs, broil for 1-2 minutes. Serve warm.

YIELD
16 artichokes

TIDBIT
President Thomas Jefferson was the first to import broccoli to America. He had seeds sent from Italy and planted them in his home farm, Monticello, in Virginia.

You can also use this recipe to stuff Portobello mushrooms.

IT'S nice to be able to pamper guests and family with more indulgent foods and desserts on a special occasion or Yom Tov. But lots of those guests also appreciate when you pull out a special dish that's also light. That's where broccoli and artichokes come together in a pretty, lemony, and satisfying dish that's also easy to prepare. And while I hope that guests pack goody bags to take home any other leftovers to enjoy another day, they can leave these for me.   –V

AHEAD: Freeze the stuffed artichokes before or after baking (step 3).

Kishka *and* Zucchini Towers

INGREDIENTS

3	large zucchini, cut into ½-inch slices
¼ cup	olive oil
•	salt to taste
•	coarse black pepper to taste

KISHKA

2 cups	flour
½ cup	breadcrumbs
¼ cup	brown sugar
1 Tbsp	paprika
2 tsp	salt
½ tsp	black pepper
⅔ cup	cold water
⅔ cup	oil

INSTRUCTIONS

1. Preheat oven to 350°F. Line 2 baking sheets with parchment paper.

2. Prepare the kishka: In a small bowl, combine flour, breadcrumbs, brown sugar, paprika, salt, and pepper. Stir in water and oil. Mold the mixture into a log that is the same width as your zucchinis. Freeze log for at least 15 minutes.

3. Place zucchini rounds on one prepared baking sheet. Remove kishka from freezer and slice into ½-inch rounds. Place kishka rounds on second prepared baking sheet.

4. Brush zucchini and kishka rounds with olive oil. Season with salt and pepper. Bake for 45-50 minutes under zucchini is tender and kishka and zucchini are golden on the edges.

5. Remove from oven. Create towers by topping a kishka round with a zucchini round, another kishka round, and a second zucchini round.

YIELD
6 servings

You can also throw this homemade kishka into your cholent.

We drizzled these towers with a tomato dip: Blend 3 tomatoes, 3 garlic cloves, 3 tablespoons olive oil, ½ teaspoon salt, and a pinch of pepper.

DURING the summertime, I like to grill slices of homemade or store-bought kishka on the barbecue. It's become such a popular dish that I adapted it into a more elegant version that I roast in the oven. Still grilling outdoors? You can grill the zucchini and kishka slices and stack them when ready for serving.

Real kishka is made using meat, but lots of brands make a pareve vegetarian version, like the one that I prepare.   -L.

AHEAD: Make the kishka ahead and keep frozen. Slice, stack, and bake fresh.

Zucchini AND Scallion Fries

INGREDIENTS

4	medium zucchini, cut into strips
4	scallions, cut in half and sliced lengthwise
2-3 Tbsp	oil
1 tsp	paprika
½ tsp	salt
½ Tbsp	onion soup mix

INSTRUCTIONS

1. Preheat oven to 425°F. Grease a baking sheet or line with parchment paper.

2. Combine zucchini and scallions on prepared baking sheet. Toss with oil, paprika, salt, and onion soup mix. Spread vegetables in a single layer. Bake until fries are soft and golden at the edges, 35-45 minutes.

YIELD
4-6 servings

To cut zucchini fries, trim off the two ends and cut the zucchini horizontally into two halves. Slice the two halves vertically down the center. Cut each quarter into strips. You'll get about 4 strips per quarter, depending on the size of the zucchini.

I'M always looking for side dishes that I can throw together in five minutes. Sometimes I'll jazz up frozen French fries with this mix of spices. This is my low-carb alternative. And while I don't usually like including an ingredient like onion soup mix in a recipe, I make an exception here. A teensy bit goes a long way.   —L.

AHEAD: Zucchini and scallion fries need to be served fresh, but you won't mind because they take only minutes to prep.

Green Bean, Basil, AND Pecan Salad

INGREDIENTS

2 lbs	green beans
1 Tbsp	olive oil
2	red onions, cut into thin strips
½ cup	chopped pecans, toasted

DRESSING

2 Tbsp	minced fresh basil
3 Tbsp	apple cider vinegar
1 Tbsp	olive oil
3	garlic cloves, minced
2 tsp	salt
•	pinch coarse black pepper

INSTRUCTIONS

1. Bring a large pot of water to a boil. Add green beans and blanch for 2 minutes. Drain; rinse beans with cold water until the steam is no longer rising from them.

2. Heat oil in a sauté pan over medium heat. Add red onions and sauté until caramelized and deeply golden, 15-20 minutes. Remove from heat and let cool.

3. Prepare the dressing: In a small bowl, combine basil, vinegar, oil, garlic, salt, and pepper.

4. In a large bowl or large plastic container, toss green beans and red onions with dressing. (If using a container with lid, place the lid on and shake it up). For best results, cover tightly and marinate in the refrigerator for up to 24 hours.

5. Top with pecans before serving.

Once you have made these over and over, you may want to change it up a bit. Use different flavored vinegars (like tarragon) or nuts (like hazelnuts) in the variations.

YIELD
8 servings

TIDBIT:
Yemenite Jews use basil as besamim (spices) for Havdalah. It is also used as a perfume on joyous occasions such as weddings.

AFTER my sister-in-law Janel brought home her new baby girl, the neighbors pitched in to make dinner for her family. On night one, they enjoyed chicken, rice, and green beans. On night two ... chicken, rice, and green beans. Yup, same goes for night three. By night four, my brother and sister-in-law were laughing while eating their chicken, rice, and green beans. Janel commented, "Too many people think that string beans need tons of oil ... but I don't want to eat greasy green beans. I want to feel good eating them."

Your wish is my command.   –V.

AHEAD: Although the flavor of these green beans will get better and better after two or three days in the fridge, they'll lose their bright green color. Serve them after a few hours or up to one day, either cold or at room temperature, for peak color and taste.

Golden Cauliflower AND Plum Tomatoes

INGREDIENTS

- 1 (24-oz) bag frozen cauliflower
- 2 plum tomatoes, chopped
- 1½ Tbsp olive oil
- 1 garlic clove, crushed
- 1½ tsp cumin
- ¼ tsp turmeric
- • pinch crushed red pepper
- 1 tsp salt
- • pinch coarse black pepper
- • juice of ½ lemon

INSTRUCTIONS

1. Preheat oven to 450°F. Line a baking sheet with parchment paper.

2. Combine cauliflower and plum tomatoes on prepared baking sheet. Toss with olive oil, garlic, cumin, turmeric, crushed red pepper, salt, and pepper.

3. Bake for 25 minutes. Sprinkle with lemon juice and serve warm.

YIELD
4 servings

INSPIRED BY COOKKOSHER MEMBER
lafayette22

TIDBIT:
Cumin has been used to spice food for as long as 5,000 years. It is mentioned in Tanach in Isaiah 28:25 as being a spice for bread.

Not in the mood for Middle Eastern flavor? Swap the cumin and turmeric for basil and oregano.

MY favorite no-fuss side dish during the week is roasted broccoli or cauliflower. I just open a bag, throw the veggies onto a baking sheet, and toss them with whichever spices coordinate with the flavors of the dinner that night. This version makes roasted cauliflower a bit more special with more than a bit more flavor — all in the same 3-minute prep time.

–V.

AHEAD: Though you can freeze or refrigerate this cauliflower and reheat in the oven, this dish comes together in just a couple of minutes. To avoid mushy cauliflower, keep the florets spread out on a baking sheet, rather than mushed together in a baking pan.

Crispy Crunchy Onion Rings

INGREDIENTS

2	medium onions (or 1 large sweet onion)
½ cup	cornstarch
¼ cup	flour
½ tsp	paprika
1 tsp	garlic powder
1½ tsp	salt
•	pinch coarse black pepper
½ cup	water
1½ cups	panko crumbs
•	oil, for frying

INSTRUCTIONS

1. Peel and slice onions into ½-inch rounds. Separate the rings. If your onions have very thin layers, keep two rings together. You don't want your onion rings to be limp.

2. In a shallow bowl, combine cornstarch, flour, paprika, garlic powder, salt, and pepper. Stir in water to form a thick paste (resist the temptation to add more water).

3. Place the panko crumbs into a second shallow bowl.

4. Add an onion ring to the batter and use a spoon to help coat. Dip onion ring in the panko crumbs and use a spoon to help coat completely.

5. Heat 2 inches of oil in a saucepan. When oil is hot, add onion rings and fry for 2-3 minutes. You do not need to flip the rings. Drain on paper towels and serve hot.

YIELD
16-18 rings

These rings deserve better than ketchup. Serve them with sweet chili sauce or the honey-garlic dipping sauce on page 85.

CRISPY, crispy onion rings. Did I mention that these are crispy? Panko is by far the crispiest crumb there is. You don't have to go with panko, though. You can use cornflake crumbs instead. But if you really want that crunch crunch crunch, get those panko crumbs into your pantry. —L.

AHEAD: After frying and draining, spread rings on a baking sheet and freeze. To reheat, spread them on a baking sheet and heat, uncovered, in a preheated oven for about 10 minutes.

Sticky Red Potatoes

INGREDIENTS

- 4-5 medium red or Yukon Gold potatoes, cut into wedges
- ½ tsp chili powder
- 2 Tbsp ketchup
- ½ tsp salt, plus more to taste
- 2 Tbsp oil

STICKY SAUCE

- 2 Tbsp oil
- 2 Tbsp ketchup
- 4 tsp vinegar
- 2 garlic cloves, crushed
- 3 Tbsp honey
- ½ tsp chili powder

INSTRUCTIONS

1. Preheat oven to 400°F. Grease a baking sheet.

2. Add potatoes to baking sheet. Add chili powder, ketchup, ½ teaspoon salt, and oil and toss to combine. Spread potatoes in a single layer and bake for 45-55 minutes.

3. Meanwhile, prepare the sticky sauce: In a small saucepan over medium heat, combine oil, ketchup, vinegar, garlic, honey, and chili powder. Cook until well combined, 3-4 minutes.

4. Toss potatoes with sticky sauce. Return potatoes to the oven for an additional 5-10 minutes. Season with additional salt to taste.

Want to fry these potatoes, as seen in the photo? Replace the oil in the sauce with a tablespoon of cornstarch. Toss fried potatoes with the sauce.

YIELD
4 servings

TIDBIT:
Some chassidim have a custom to make the blessing of she'hakol on potatoes, even though they are vegetables. That's because potatoes are similar to mushrooms, as they receive nutrients from water. The second reason is because of the potato's versatility. Because it can also be used as a flour, like a grain, she'hakol is said to avoid doubt over whether to say ha'adamah or mezonos.

ONE Friday, I prepared a pan of these potatoes to enjoy Shabbos night. When I entered my kitchen before candle lighting, I peeked inside the pan. There were only five little potato wedges left! This was one of my side dishes and there was no time to make more (don't worry, I had plenty of kugel)! The little fingerprints left in the pan helped me narrow down the list of culprits. None of the kids, though, would admit to eating more than one or two. Hard to believe. Since there were only five left, I kept the remainder for myself. I'm sure everyone else already had their share.   –L.

AHEAD: These potatoes are best prepared the same day. If preparing earlier in the day, don't refrigerate. Keep at room temperature and reheat before serving.

New Potatoes with Spinach

INGREDIENTS

3 lbs	assorted new (mini) potatoes, halved
¼ cup	olive oil
2 tsp	minced onion
1 tsp	garlic powder
2 tsp	salt
¼ tsp	coarse black pepper
6 oz	(4 cups) fresh spinach

INSTRUCTIONS

1. Preheat oven to 425°F.

2. On a baking sheet, combine potatoes, olive oil, minced onion, garlic powder, salt, and pepper. Bake for 40-45 minutes.

3. Toss spinach with potatoes on the baking sheet. Return to oven and bake for an additional 8-10 minutes. Taste and season with more salt, if necessary, and serve.

YIELD
6 servings

TIDBIT:
The popular belief that spinach adds strength is due to a mistaken measurement taken in 1870 that showed spinach to have 10 times its actual iron content. Spinach has no more iron than other green leafy vegetables.

A couple of years ago, a writer for a weekly food magazine featured a recipe that included blue potatoes. I objected. I thought that blue potatoes were not an accessible product and felt that it's hard for readers when we present recipes that use ingredients we can't find. Of course, the reader can go ahead and use regular potatoes, but it's still a tease. I also thought that blue potatoes were a fad and would soon go the way of green ketchup.

Now, blue potatoes are sold in my local vegetable market and even in ... Costco! Looks like they are here to stay. Let's embrace them!

–L.

AHEAD: These potatoes are best prepared the same day. You can roast the potatoes earlier in the day. Before serving, toss with spinach and roast for the final few minutes.

PLATE IT!

Use your extra butternut squash purée to plate the Winter Squash Ravioli (page 50).

1 Place scallions in a bowl of ice water and watch them curl up.

2 Place some reserved butternut squash purée on your appetizer plate. Use the back of a spoon to make a circular indentation in the center.

3 Place a few raviolis into the center of the purée.

4 Top with curly scallions and serve.

GRAINS

Focaccia with Roasted Vegetables

INGREDIENTS

DOUGH

1 cup	whole wheat flour
¾ cup	flour
1 tsp	salt
2 tsp	sugar
1 tsp	active dry yeast
1 cup	water (or as needed)
2 tsp	olive oil

ROASTED VEGETABLES

2½-3 cups	total diced sweet potatoes, eggplants, and zucchini
¼ cup	olive oil
¾ tsp	salt
•	pinch coarse black pepper

FOCACCIA TOPPING

1½ Tbsp	olive oil
2	garlic cloves, minced
½	scallion, diced
¼ tsp	dried oregano
¼ tsp	dried basil
¼ tsp	kosher salt

INSTRUCTIONS

1. Prepare the dough: In the bowl of an electric mixer, combine flours, salt, sugar, and yeast. Stir to combine. Add water, a little bit at a time, while mixing, until a dough forms. Add oil and mix to combine. Form dough into a ball and place into a greased bowl. Cover and let rise for 30-40 minutes. If the dough is sticky, coat with a bit of flour when forming into a ball, but don't add more flour to the dough.

2. Preheat oven to 475°F. On the bottom rack, place a pizza stone or an upside-down baking sheet. Line a second baking sheet with aluminum foil.

3. Prepare the vegetables: Toss vegetables with olive oil, salt, and pepper. Spread on lined baking sheet. Place baking sheet into the top half of the oven and roast for 25 minutes. Set aside.

4. Stretch dough into a flat oval on a sheet of parchment paper. Brush with olive oil and top with garlic, scallions, oregano, and basil. Place onto hot pizza stone or upside-down baking sheet. Bake for 13 minutes. (This may be done while the vegetables are roasting.)

5. To serve, top focaccia with roasted vegetables and sprinkle with salt.

We like the rustic look of the whole wheat focaccia, but you can also use all white flour.

YIELD
4 servings

TIDBIT: In the 18th century, the most common variety of eggplant in Europe was small, white, and round, resembling large eggs. The name stuck even though the elongated wine-colored variety is more common today.

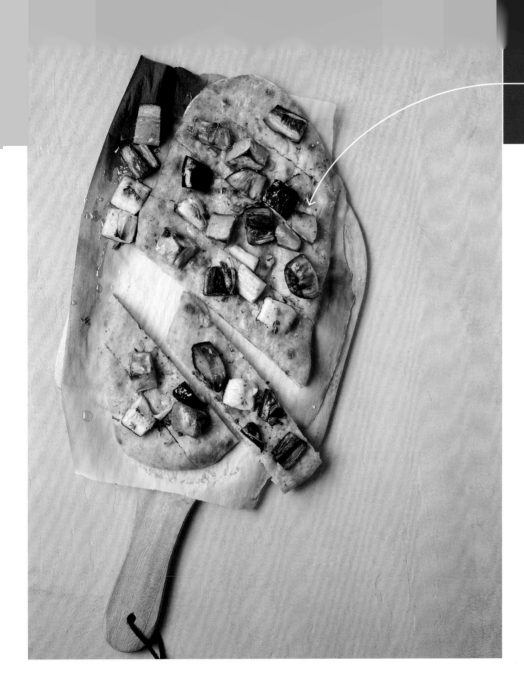

Don't forget this finishing salt. Coarse sea salt will also work well (but not table salt!).

MANY people have gotten into the habit of taking photos of the food they order when dining out. Some restaurants don't like it, since the food doesn't look that great when photographed under dim lights. Yet I love it. Friends and family around the world know that I love to see what they've enjoyed lately. My sister-in-law sent me a photo of this dish while dining out in Israel. The next day, it was on my table, too.   —L.

AHEAD: Nothing is like fresh bread! For the best of both worlds, you can freeze balls of dough and bake fresh. The roasted vegetables can be prepared earlier in the day.

Winter Squash Ravioli

INGREDIENTS

1	(2½ lbs) narrow butternut squash
1 Tbsp	olive oil
1	large sweet onion, diced
1 Tbsp	salt
36	(3-inch) ravioli rounds
•	oil, for toasting

HERB SAUCE

¼ cup	olive oil
¼ cup	minced garlic cloves (10-12 cloves)
2 tsp	dried thyme
2 tsp	dried parsley flakes

INSTRUCTIONS

1. Prepare the ravioli: Preheat oven to 400°F. Place butternut squash into a baking pan and bake for 60-80 minutes, rotating halfway through (a thick squash may need more time). Squash should be completely soft. Let cool completely. Discard peel and seeds and add the butternut squash flesh to a medium bowl.

2. Heat olive oil in a sauté pan over medium-low heat. Add onion and sauté until golden and caramelized, about 20 minutes.

3. Add onions and salt to the butternut squash. Using an immersion blender, blend until completely smooth.

4. Place a teaspoon of squash onto each ravioli round. Fold in half and seal tightly closed, then pinch the two edges together (see photo). Reserve any remaining squash purée.

5. Heat oil in a large sauté pan over medium heat. Add ravioli in batches and cook until golden, about 3 minutes per side. Set aside.

6. Prepare the herb sauce: Heat olive oil in a sauté pan over medium heat. Add garlic, thyme, and parsley. Cook until garlic is golden, 1-2 minutes. Toss with raviolis.

7. To serve, spoon some reserved purée onto each dish; top with raviolis. Garnish with fresh thyme and parsley (optional). To make a smoother purée, press squash through a wire strainer or sieve.

YIELD
36 raviolis

You can also use store-bought ravioli rounds to make kreplach.

See Plate It! on page 46 to see how we plated this pretty pasta.

I'M usually very partial to home-made dough. But not when it comes to ravioli. Then, I am very happy to grab the package of ravioli dough rounds from the freezer section, and my pasta dish is ready in as long as it takes a pot of water to boil. I usually stuff ravioli rounds with a shredded cheese and egg mixture to make *calsones*, a traditional Syrian dish, where the raviolis are boiled with egg noodles, then tossed with butter and baked. Those reliable ravioli rounds, though, are ready for an upgrade with this dreamy pareve butternut squash version. The house smells so good when I'm preparing it ... and it just may be my family's new favorite ravioli dish. −V.

AHEAD: Raviolis are the perfect freezer-friendly pasta. Freeze them after step 4. When ready to serve, pull some out of the freezer, let thaw, and complete steps 5-7 for a quick gourmet pasta dish.

Barbecue Noodles

INGREDIENTS

2-3 Tbsp	oil
1	large onion, cut into thin strips
3	garlic cloves, crushed
2 cups	shredded green cabbage
1	red pepper, sliced
1	(15-oz) can bean sprouts
1	carrot, julienned
3 tsp	salt
1 tsp	paprika
½ tsp	chili powder
1 tsp	mustard
2 tsp	brown sugar
½ cup	barbecue sauce
1 lb	fettuccine, prepared according to package directions
1 Tbsp	chopped fresh parsley

INSTRUCTIONS

1. Heat oil in a sauté pan over medium heat. Add onion and garlic and sauté for 5 minutes. Add cabbage, red pepper, bean sprouts, and carrot and sauté for an additional 2-3 minutes.

2. Add salt, paprika, chili powder, mustard, brown sugar, and barbecue sauce and mix well. Stir in noodles and cook for an additional 2 minutes. Stir in parsley.

Use your favorite BBQ sauce. Honey garlic is a great choice.

YIELD
6-8 servings

If you can purchase fresh bean sprouts, use them instead!

FETTUCCINE is the kind of pasta that you pair with an Alfredo sauce. But what kind of fettuccine can we serve for a meat dinner? Well, any good barbecue dinner deserves a just-as-good barbecue noodles as a side dish. And don't worry; you won't have to make more room on the grill.　　　－L.

AHEAD: You can prepare this pasta earlier in the day and serve at room temperature. Or, sauté the vegetables and boil the pasta the night before and continue with step 2 when ready to serve.

Sesame Orzo

INGREDIENTS

1 Tbsp	oil
1 cup	orzo
2½ cups	chicken stock
2 Tbsp	soy sauce
1 tsp	sugar
1	garlic clove, crushed
2 Tbsp	sesame oil
1-2	scallions, sliced
•	sesame seeds, for garnish

INSTRUCTIONS

1. Heat oil in a sauté pan over high heat. Add orzo and toast until some of the pasta has browned, 1-2 minutes.

2. Add chicken stock, soy sauce, sugar, and garlic. Bring to a boil. Lower heat to medium-low and simmer, stirring occasionally, until liquid is mostly absorbed, 20-25 minutes. Remove from heat and stir in sesame oil, scallions, and sesame seeds.

YIELD
4 servings

Sesame oil is always added in at the end. While this oil has a lot of flavor, it has a low smoke point, so it isn't best to use it for cooking or frying. Use a bit in salad dressings or drizzle on top of roasted Asian veggies.

ORZO is one of the easiest pastas to dress up. Sauté vegetables such as spinach, tomatoes, or mushrooms ... or even just onions with strips of pastrami. Just make sure to add a little oil and some spices. But you don't need a recipe for that ... that's the type of dish that varies according to your mood or what's in your produce drawer. So why this recipe? Two reasons. Loads of flavor. One pot.   —L.

AHEAD: If you want to prepare this in advance, you'll need to add more oil when reheating to keep the pasta from drying out.

Couscous AND Crumbs

INGREDIENTS

- **1** (8.8-oz) package Israeli couscous, prepared according to package directions
- **2** zucchinis, sliced into half-moons
- **4 Tbsp** oil, divided
- **1 tsp** salt, plus more to taste
- **1 tsp** cumin
- **1 tsp** dried basil
- **1 tsp** garlic powder
- **2 Tbsp** cornflake crumbs
- **2 tsp** lemon juice
- **1-2** garlic cloves, crushed
- • pinch coarse black pepper to taste

INSTRUCTIONS

1. Preheat oven to 425°F. Grease a baking sheet or line with parchment paper.

2. On prepared baking sheet, toss zucchini with 1 tablespoon oil, 1 teaspoon salt, cumin, basil, and garlic powder. Spread in a single layer and bake for 15-20 minutes, until beginning to turn golden.

3. Heat 2 tablespoons oil in a sauté pan over medium heat. Add cornflake crumbs and sauté until toasted and crisp, about 2 minutes.

4. In a medium bowl, toss couscous with cornflake crumbs, zucchini, lemon juice, garlic, pepper, and remaining 1 tablespoon oil. Season with additional salt to taste.

YIELD
4 servings

TIDBIT:
In Israel, Israeli couscous is called p'titim. The Italians call it acini di pepe, which means "peppercorns." Victoria grew up eating Israeli couscous in a dish she calls keskesoon.

DIFFERENT shapes of pasta really do taste different. What?!? You don't agree? I know it's all just flour and water, but those different textures really do play with our taste buds. Take Israeli couscous. Even though it's technically pasta, those little balls have their own personality.   —L.

AHEAD: Although best fresh, this dish can be prepared up to a few days in advance and served at room temperature or briefly reheated. Taste and adjust seasonings and oil before serving.

Three-Onion Brown Rice

INGREDIENTS

2 cups	short grain brown rice
3 Tbsp	oil
2	large sweet onions, diced
10	shallots, diced
3	thick leeks, white and light green parts only, sliced into rings
2 tsp	salt, or to taste
•	pinch coarse black pepper

INSTRUCTIONS

1. Prepare rice according to package instructions.

2. While rice is cooking, heat oil in a large sauté pan over medium-low heat. Add onions and shallots and sauté until beginning to soften, about 5 minutes. Add leeks and continue to cook, stirring occasionally, until onions are completely caramelized and golden, about 40 minutes.

3. Add onions to the rice and stir to combine. Remove from heat and let steam for 10 minutes with the lid on. The rice will have a creamy risotto-like consistency. Fluff with a fork and season with salt and pepper.

YIELD
6 servings

The berachah on rice is mezonos like for grains, and the after-berachah is borei nefashos like for vegetables. That's because rice is not one of the five grains mentioned in the Torah.

This recipe works well with white rice and wild rice too.

IT'S very hard to beat plain rice. White or brown, just give it enough oil and salt, follow the instructions on the package, and you really can't go wrong. I'm in food heaven when I'm enjoying a simple bowl of rice with coleslaw.

There is one thing, though, that will always beat plain rice. And that's rice with lots and lots of fried onions. –V.

AHEAD: You can cook all the onions ahead of time and add them to the freshly cooked rice in step 3.

Yemenite "Yellow" Orzo Rice

INGREDIENTS

3 Tbsp	olive oil
1	large onion, finely diced
4	garlic cloves, crushed
3 tsp	cumin
1½ tsp	turmeric
2 tsp	salt, or to taste
•	pinch coarse black pepper
¾ cup	orzo
1¼ cups	rice
4 cups	chicken stock

INSTRUCTIONS

1. Heat oil in a sauté pan over medium heat. Add onion; sauté until golden, 10-12 minutes. Stir in garlic, cumin, turmeric, salt, and pepper.

2. Add orzo and toast, stirring occasionally, for 4 minutes. Add uncooked rice and stir for an additional 3 minutes.

3. Add chicken stock. Raise heat and bring to a boil. Lower heat, cover, and simmer until liquid is absorbed, 18-20 minutes. Remove from heat and let steam (with the cover on) for 10 minutes. Fluff with a fork and serve.

YIELD
6 servings

INSPIRED BY
COOKKOSHER MEMBER
EAloof

Combining cumin and turmeric give this rice a sweet flavor, but if you're not feeling brave, start with a little less spice.

Mixing the rice with orzo gives this dish a great texture.

IT all started when my guests called the red cabbage salad the "purple salad." After that, my kids dismissed all my attempts to call food by its proper name. Spanish rice is now called "red rice," and this Yemenite rice is "yellow rice." If I called it Yemenite rice, they probably wouldn't want to eat it, but "yellow rice" is all they want to eat! It's all about the marketing.   –L.

AHEAD: Rice is usually best prepared fresh but this rice reheats well in a microwave.

Forbidden Black Rice WITH Mango and Peaches

INGREDIENTS

1 cup	Forbidden black rice
2 Tbsp	oil
4	garlic cloves, crushed
1	mango, diced
2	peaches, diced
½	red onion, finely diced
•	juice of 2 limes (about 3 Tbsp)
10	fresh mint leaves, chopped
¾ tsp	salt, or to taste

INSTRUCTIONS

1. Prepare rice according to package directions.

2. Heat oil in a frying pan over medium-low heat. Add garlic and sauté until lightly golden, about 2 minutes. Stir garlic and oil into rice. Add in mango, peaches, red onion, lime juice, mint, and salt.

YIELD
4 servings

Stick to fruit that is in season. During the winter, use an additional mango instead of the peaches and add some pomegranate arils.

IF you want to bring something stunning to the table, bring home a package of Forbidden black rice. It's a type of wild rice, with a nutty flavor and a striking solid black appearance. It only takes a little longer than white rice to cook (unlike brown rice, which takes forever), but it's loads healthier. I love this refreshing, fruity version. —V.

AHEAD: *Like most rice dishes, this is best prepared fresh.*

Balsamic Quinoa Salad

INGREDIENTS

- *1 cup* quinoa
- *1* zucchini, diced
- *1* yellow squash, diced
- *1* red pepper, diced
- *½* red onion, finely diced
- *½ Tbsp* oil
- *¼ tsp* salt

DRESSING

- *½ cup* balsamic vinegar
- *¼ cup* water
- *¼ cup* olive oil
- *3 Tbsp* brown sugar
- *2 Tbsp* chopped fresh basil
- *1 tsp* salt
- • pinch coarse black pepper

INSTRUCTIONS

1. Preheat oven to 350°F. Line a baking sheet with parchment paper.

2. Bring 2 cups water to boil in a medium saucepan. Add quinoa, lower heat to low, cover, and cook for 15 minutes. Remove from heat.

3. Toss zucchini, squash, red pepper, and red onion on prepared baking sheet. Toss with oil and salt and spread in a single layer. Bake for 15 minutes, or until vegetables are softened.

4. Prepare the dressing: In a small bowl, whisk together balsamic vinegar, water, olive oil, brown sugar, basil, salt, and pepper.

5. In a medium bowl, toss quinoa, roasted vegetables and dressing.

YIELD
6-8 servings

INSPIRED BY
COOKKOSHER MEMBER
melissa

Quinoa soaks up dressing, so always use it all!

I admit, I never really loved quinoa until it came time to test recipes for this book. Sometimes, though, recipe efforts are blessed and the next Shabbat, two of the best quinoa dishes I had ever tasted were on my table. My guests and I kept on tasting both ... not only because we couldn't decide, but because both were so good! In the end, this balsamic quinoa was the winner. —V.

AHEAD: Prepare the quinoa and vegetables up to 3 days in advance and toss with the dressing before serving.

PLATE IT!

Yes, your chicken drumettes can look beautiful! Here's how we plated the Chestnut Chicken (page 88).

1 Use a mandoline to slice a potato into thin discs. Toss the potatoes with oil, salt, and basil. Stack them in muffin tins and bake until golden at the edges, 30–40 minutes.

2 Center one potato stack in the center of the plate.

3 Place one drumette on top of the potato stack and one drumette on the side. Scatter chestnuts on the plate and over the drumettes.

4 Drizzle some of the cooking sauce on the side of the dish and top with fresh herbs.

MEAT & CHICKEN

Corned Beef ᴀɴᴅ Spinach Spring Rolls

INGREDIENTS

2 Tbsp	oil
1	onion, diced
1	(16-oz) bag frozen chopped spinach
1 tsp	garlic powder
1 tsp	onion powder
¾ tsp	salt
2 Tbsp	mayonnaise
2 tsp	mustard
⅛ tsp	black pepper
12	spring roll wrappers
6 oz	deli corned beef, cut into thin strips
1 tsp	cornstarch dissolved in 3 Tbsp water

DIPPING SAUCE

2 tsp	yellow mustard
¼ cup	mayonnaise
1 Tbsp	brown sugar

INSTRUCTIONS

1. Heat oil in a sauté pan over medium-high heat. Add onion and sauté until completely soft, about 7 minutes. Add spinach and continue to sauté until spinach is completely cooked, about 15 minutes. Add garlic powder, onion powder, salt, mayonnaise, mustard, and black pepper.

2. Place a spring roll wrapper on your work surface. Shape 1½ tablespoons of spinach mixture into a log-shaped mound in the center of the wrapper. Place 1½ tablespoons corned beef over spinach mixture. Fold in the two sides, then fold the bottom half of the wrapper over the filling. Roll up to completely enclose. Brush the top edge with a bit of the cornstarch mixture to seal. Spring rolls can be frozen at this point.

3. To bake the spring rolls, preheat oven to 425°F. Line a baking sheet with aluminum foil and grease with nonstick cooking spray. Place spring rolls on the sheet, leaving space between them. Spray the tops and sides with nonstick cooking spray. Bake for 18 minutes, or until crispy. (Alternatively, you can fry the spring rolls: Heat 1-2 inches oil in a saucepan. When hot, add spring rolls and fry until crispy, 3-4 minutes per side.)

4. Prepare the dipping sauce: In a small microwave-safe dish, combine mustard, mayonnaise, and brown sugar. Stir to combine. Microwave for 30 seconds, or until sugar has dissolved. Stir again. Serve with spring rolls.

YIELD
12 spring rolls

TIDBIT:
Corned beef takes its name, not from corn, but rather because it is pickled in brine made with "corns" — coarse grains — of salt. In the UK, corned beef is known as salt beef.

Keep this recipe pareve by omitting the corned beef. Or even better ... swap out the meat for cheese if you want to serve these at a dairy meal.

GIVE me a spring roll, and I'll eat it. I've stuffed them with avocado, brisket, vegetables .... I've even stuffed these wrappers with brownies and fried them for dessert. These, though, are my best spring rolls yet. Of course, they're better fried, but these also actually work very well when they are baked.   –L.

AHEAD: The spring rolls will freeze well. Freeze raw after step 2 and bake or fry fresh. You can also prepare the dipping sauce in advance and refrigerate. Let it come to room temperature before serving.

Crispy Beef

INGREDIENTS

1¼ lbs	shoulder steak or London broil, cut into thin slices
¼ cup	cornstarch, for marinade
1 tsp	salt
•	pinch coarse black pepper
•	oil, for frying
1-2 Tbsp	cornstarch
1	onion, cut into thin strips
2	garlic cloves, crushed
½	red pepper, diced

SAUCE

¼ cup	soy sauce
2 Tbsp	rice vinegar
1½ Tbsp	honey
4 Tbsp	brown sugar
½ tsp	chili powder (or up to 1 tsp if you like it spicier)
1½ tsp	cornstarch dissolved in ¼ cup water

INSTRUCTIONS

1. In a medium bowl, combine meat, ¼ cup cornstarch, salt, and pepper. Marinate 30 minutes at room temperature.

2. Heat 2-3 inches oil in a saucepan or deep fryer over medium-high heat. Right before frying, toss meat with an additional 1-2 tablespoons cornstarch. Add meat and fry until cooked through, about 2 minutes per side. Remove meat from pan and set aside.

3. Prepare the sauce: In a small bowl, whisk together soy sauce, rice vinegar, honey, brown sugar, chili powder, and cornstarch mixture. Set aside.

4. Pour out most of the oil from the saucepan, leaving only 1 tablespoon. Heat pan over medium heat. Add onion, garlic, and red pepper and sauté until onion is beginning to soften but still crunchy, about 5 minutes. Add in sauce and beef and cook an additional 2 minutes, until warmed through.

YIELD
6-8 servings

INSPIRED BY COOKKOSHER MEMBER
chef1

To make the savory fortune cookie pictured, fold a round dumpling wrapper in half and pinch the edges together without flattening the wrapper. Pinch the two ends together. Secure with a toothpick and deep-fry.

Letting the beef sit in a cornstarch mixture is part of the "velveting" process that Chinese restaurants use to tenderize meat.

WHILE researching for this book, we asked lots of people what types of appetizers they love. We had many requests for crispy beef, which is thin strips of beef tossed with a sauce and is popular in American-Chinese restaurants. Thanks for reminding us! We love it too! Luckily, a cookkosher member had already shared her version. We tested and tweaked, and with some tips from a Chinese takeout owner, here it is.   –L.

AHEAD: You can fry the beef early in the day. Toss and heat it with the sauce when ready to serve.

Braised Steak Kebabs *with* Apricots

INGREDIENTS

1¼ lbs	minute steak roast, cut into ¾-inch cubes
1	onion, cut into strips
36	dried apricots
36	dried cherries or prunes
½ tsp	salt
•	pinch coarse black pepper
12 oz	beer

MARINADE

1 cup	pomegranate juice
½ cup	teriyaki sauce
2	garlic cloves, crushed
¼ cup	olive oil

INSTRUCTIONS

1. Prepare the marinade: In a medium bowl, combine pomegranate juice, teriyaki sauce, garlic, and olive oil. Add steak cubes. Cover and marinate in the refrigerator for 4-6 hours or up to overnight.

2. Preheat oven to 350°F. Place onion strips into a Dutch oven or roasting pan.

3. Remove steak cubes from marinade (reserve marinade) and thread skewers with steak cubes, apricots, and cherries or prunes. Place skewers over onions and season with salt and pepper.

4. Pour beer and reserved marinade over skewers. Cover and bake for 1½ hours.

YIELD
18 skewers

Why minute steak? It's a cut of meat that is best prepared by braising.

SOME people will tell you that kebabs belong only on the grill. Don't tell that to the Jewish homemaker, who does not want to be standing over a fire right before a meal, but still wants to bring these pretty, juicy, and flavorful bites to the table. Kebabs that we can throw into the oven and then pull out and serve are way more practical. These kebabs are marinated and then braised, giving the meat plenty of time to absorb its fruity (but not overly sweet) marinade. I think that my skewers have found a brand-new home: in a roasting pan. 　　　　　　 –V.

AHEAD: These kebabs will freeze well after cooking; just make sure they have plenty of liquid to keep from drying out when reheating.

Tangy Meat Pizzas (Lehme B'agine)

INGREDIENTS

DOUGH

1 tsp	dry yeast
1¼ cups	warm water, divided
2 Tbsp	sugar
4 cups	flour
1 tsp	salt
2 Tbsp	oil

TOPPING

1 cup	prune butter
¾ cup	ketchup
¼ cup	tomato paste
¼ cup	lemon juice
1	onion, very finely diced
1 tsp	cinnamon
1 tsp	allspice
1 tsp	garlic powder
1½ tsp	salt
½ tsp	coarse black pepper
1-1⅓ lbs	ground beef

INSTRUCTIONS

1. Prepare the dough: In a large bowl, dissolve yeast in warm water with sugar. Add flour, salt, and oil, and knead until a soft dough forms. Let rise for 1 hour.

2. Preheat oven to 350°F. Line 2 baking sheets with parchment paper.

3. Roll out dough to ¼-inch thickness. Cut rounds using a cookie cutter or drinking glass. Place on prepared baking sheets. If preparing dough rounds in advance, keep them frozen until ready to use.

4. Prepare the meat topping: In a medium bowl, combine prune butter, ketchup, tomato paste, lemon juice, onion, cinnamon, allspice, garlic powder, salt, and pepper. Add ground meat, a little bit at a time, mixing very well, until completely combined.

5. Top dough rounds with a generous amount of the meat mixture (overestimate, as the rounds will grow in the oven while the meat shrinks). Bake until bottoms of rounds are lightly browned, about 25 minutes. Serve with chummus or techineh. (We also garnished with fresh parsley and tomato pulp. See photo.)

YIELD
24 lehme b'agine

Want to save time? Here's the secret to making your store-bought dough taste almost like homemade. Place the mini dough rounds on the baking sheets; thaw completely and let rise for at least 2 hours before topping with meat and baking. The same trick will also work when you're using the dough to make mini pizzas.

Although tamarind syrup is the authentic ingredient, prune butter is a more accessible and very successful substitute.

OF all Syrian mazzeh (hors d'oeuvres), lehme b'agine is probably the Ashkenaz Jew's favorite. It's also the easiest to make, especially if you use store-bought dough (choose mini pizza doughs). Leah tells me that one of her neighbors even serves it as an appetizer on Shabbat (gefilte fish, are you jealous?). In my house, there is no fish course at Shabbat meals. Rather, the mazzeh (including this lehme b'agine) is on the table at the start of the meal. And, no, there was no ketchup in Aleppo. But that doesn't mean that authentic is always best. This is the secret sauce recipe that my sister-in-law Rachel received from a caterer. Now, I am permitted to share. –V.

AHEAD: Fill your freezer with unbaked lehme b'agine. Just pop them in the oven the day of serving.

Falafel Cigars

INGREDIENTS

2 Tbsp	olive oil
1	large onion, finely diced
½ lb	ground meat
2 Tbsp	falafel mix
1 tsp	salt
5	(10-inch) whole wheat wraps
6 Tbsp	chummus or techineh
2 cups	prepared coleslaw
1	egg, beaten
•	oil, for browning

INSTRUCTIONS

1. Heat oil in a sauté pan over medium heat. Add onion and sauté until soft, about 5-7 minutes. Add meat and brown, pressing with a fork to break up the clumps. Stir in falafel mix and salt.

2. Cut wraps into four segments, like pizza wedges. Place the rounded edge of a wedge facing you, with the pointy tip facing away. Spread a layer of chummus along the bottom-center, about 1-inch from the bottom and sides. Top with layer of meat. Top meat with coleslaw. Keep the filling in a long, thin strip for nicely shaped cigars.

3. Fold in the two sides over the filling. Fold the bottom up over the filling, and holding the filling in place with your fingers, roll up tightly, jelly-roll style. Brush tip of wrap with beaten egg to seal.

4. Heat a thin layer of oil in a sauté pan over medium heat. When oil is hot, add cigars, seam side down, and cook until golden brown, turning once, about 1 minute per side.

To make your own slaw, combine ¼ cup mayonnaise, 2 tablespoons vinegar, 2 tablespoons water, and 2 teaspoons sugar. Add in 2 cups shredded cabbage, a little at a time, and toss to combine.

YIELD
20 cigars

TIDBIT:
The origin of the word falafel is likely the Aramaic word "pilpel." The same word is also used in Hebrew. It means pepper, and the name could be derived from the falafel ball's similarity in shape and taste to peppercorns.

Can't find falafel mix? Spice the meat with cumin, garlic, and parsley.

WE had been dreaming about stuffing the flavors of a falafel sandwich into a neat, compact hors d'oeuvre-style cigar for a while. I finally devoted one morning to making it happen. By afternoon, these were all ready in a bowl on the counter. Everyone around starting grabbing them for lunch. I had to act fast before they were gone: Should I eat meat so early in the day and give up the chance to have something cheesy later?

I did it. I ate one. And my eyes lit up. Such a satisfying, delicious bite! Now, I don't ever hesitate to be "meat" when these are around.

–V.

AHEAD: You can freeze these cigars after rolling. Simply thaw before browning them in the sauté pan. You can also brown them ahead of time, freeze, then thaw, and reheat on a hot plate.

Veal-Stuffed Mushrooms

INGREDIENTS

24 oz	whole baby bella mushrooms, divided
1	egg
1 cup	seasoned breadcrumbs
2 Tbsp	olive oil
2 Tbsp	red wine vinegar
½ tsp	salt, or to taste
•	pinch coarse black pepper
•	oil, for frying

FILLING

1	onion, cut into chunks
2 Tbsp	olive oil
3	garlic cloves, minced
2 tsp	chopped fresh basil
¾ lb	ground veal
1½ tsp	salt
•	pinch coarse black pepper

INSTRUCTIONS

1. Sort the mushrooms. Set aside the largest, nicest mushrooms for stuffing and remove the stems. The mushrooms that are too small for stuffing (about ¼ of the mushrooms) will be used in the filling.

2. Prepare the filling: In the bowl of a food processor, combine onion, small mushrooms, and mushroom stems. Pulse until finely diced.

3. Heat oil in a sauté pan over medium heat. Add onion/mushroom mixture and garlic and sauté 5-7 minutes. Stir in basil. In a medium bowl, combine mixture with veal and season with salt and pepper.

4. Lightly beat egg in a small bowl. Place breadcrumbs into a second small bowl. Stuff each mushroom with a mound of the veal mixture. Dip stuffed mushrooms into egg and then into breadcrumbs.

5. Preheat oven to 350°F. Add olive oil and vinegar to a baking pan.

6. Heat oil in a sauté pan over medium-high heat. Add mushrooms, stuffing side down, and fry until bread-crumb topping is crispy and golden, 3-4 minutes. Add the fried mushrooms to prepared baking pan. Season with additional salt and pepper. Bake until mushrooms are cooked through, about 20 minutes.

YIELD
24-30 mushrooms

TIDBIT:
Even though mushrooms grow in the ground, they receive their nutrients from water, not the soil. That's why the blessing on mushrooms is she'hakol, not ha'adamah.

You'll see that baby bellas are our mushroom of choice throughout this book. They give you the flavor of Portobellos, at a price that's comparable to white buttons.

AT my family's Purim *seudah*, everyone prepares a dish or two. I brought these to my mother-in-law's house a couple of days in advance so they'd be there on time (while I, of course, arrive late) and provided cooking instructions. When I finally finished delivering all my *mishloach manot* late Purim afternoon, I made my entrance. When I opened the door, I received a very warm greeting: "The veal mushrooms! The veal mushrooms!"

I suppose that means they were popular.   –V.

AHEAD: You can freeze the mushrooms after frying (or refrigerate for up to 2 days). Complete step 6 when ready to serve. If your mushrooms are completely frozen, they may need a few extra minutes of baking time.

Sweetbreads WITH White Wine-Parsley Sauce

INGREDIENTS

1 lb	veal sweetbreads
1 Tbsp	vinegar
⅓ cup	cornmeal
2-3 Tbsp	oil
½ cup	dry white wine
1 Tbsp	honey
¼ tsp	salt
•	pinch coarse black pepper
2 Tbsp	chopped fresh parsley or 2 tsp dried parsley, divided

INSTRUCTIONS

1. Soak sweetbreads in water for 2 hours and drain. Rinse well.

2. Place sweetbreads, 2 cups water, and vinegar into a medium saucepan. Bring to a boil and cook until sweetbreads are opaque, about 25 minutes. Drain and rinse under cold water. Remove membranes (see note).

3. Place cornmeal into a wide bowl. Add the sweetbreads and toss to coat.

4. Heat oil in a sauté pan over medium-high heat. When oil is hot, add sweetbreads and cook until golden and crusty, about 2 minutes per side. Remove from pan and set aside.

5. Lower heat to medium. Pour wine into sauté pan, deglazing the pan. Bring to a simmer. Add honey, salt, pepper, and half the parsley. Cook until wine is slightly reduced, 3-4 minutes. Spoon sauce over sweetbreads before serving. Garnish with remaining parsley.

Many butchers sell sweetbreads with the membranes already removed. If your sweetbreads still contain the membranes, carefully peel them away after boiling. Make sure to wait until the sweetbreads are cool enough to handle.

YIELD
4 servings

To complete the presentation, serve these sweetbreads over 2 puff pastry triangles or rectangles or toast points. Slice 8 puff pastry squares or 8 crustless slices of bread into triangles. Brush with olive oil and bake at 375°F for 10 minutes.

I love shopping in kitchen supply stores. I don't own too many gadgets, but I still find shops like The Peppermill in Brooklyn very inspiring. Last time I was there, the owners showed me one of their new products: a lemon spray. You stick it into a fresh lemon and it transforms the fruit into a spray bottle. Just press the nozzle and fresh lemon juice spritzes out. And while I don't need a lemon sprayer, I do need this recipe for sweetbreads, which the owners at The Peppermill shared with me. It's perfect for the gourmet diner in your life.   –L.

AHEAD: Sweetbreads can be prepared through step 2 and refrigerated or frozen. Continue with step 3 when ready to cook.

Shwarma Egg Rolls

INGREDIENTS

3 Tbsp	oil, divided, plus more for frying
1	onion, cut into thin strips
1¼ lbs	boneless chicken thighs or breast, cut into strips
1 tsp	paprika
1 tsp	cumin
¾ tsp	allspice
½ tsp	turmeric
½ tsp	garlic powder
½ tsp	salt
•	pinch chili powder
8	egg roll wrappers

INSTRUCTIONS

1. Heat 2 tablespoons oil in a large sauté pan over medium heat. Add onion and sauté for 3-4 minutes. Push onions to the side of the pan and add chicken strips. Sauté until chicken is cooked through and white, 8-10 minutes.

2. Add remaining 1 tablespoon oil, paprika, cumin, allspice, turmeric, garlic powder, salt, and chili powder; toss to combine.

3. Place the egg roll wrapper with one point facing you. Add chicken to the bottom-center of each egg roll wrapper. Fold in half on the diagonal, forming a triangle. Wet the edges of the wrapper to help seal it.

4. Heat 2 inches oil in a small saucepan over medium-high heat. Add egg rolls and fry until golden brown, 2-3 minutes on each side.

Short on time? Use a shwarma spice blend.

YIELD
8 egg rolls

Make this a main dish! Serve the chicken filling with laffa or pita and some chummus or techineh on the side. For more main course ideas, see page 126.

SHWARMA is made from various types of meat or poultry, depending on what country you're in. Most Israeli shwarma is made from chicken thighs or turkey, or a combination of both. And while shwarma is a Middle Eastern creation, it's only in America that you can find it stuffed inside an egg roll. Maybe it's time the Israelis catch on.

—L.

AHEAD: Freeze these egg rolls after filling them and fry them fresh.

Crispy Chicken Rolls WITH Honey-Garlic Dipping Sauce

INGREDIENTS

1 Tbsp	oil, plus more for frying
1	onion, cut into very thin strips
5	(10-inch) whole wheat wraps

CHICKEN

1 lb	chicken cutlets, pounded thin
1 tsp	salt, divided
•	pinch coarse black pepper
1½ Tbsp	minced garlic, divided
¾ cup	panko crumbs
1 tsp	chili powder
¾ tsp	paprika
1	egg

RED CABBAGE SALAD

1¼ cups	red cabbage
2 Tbsp	vinegar
1 tsp	oil
¼ tsp	sugar
¼ tsp	salt

INSTRUCTIONS

1. Heat oil in a sauté pan over medium heat. Add onion and sauté until soft and lightly golden, about 10 minutes. Set aside.

2. Season chicken with ½ teaspoon salt, pepper, and ½ tablespoon minced garlic.

3. In a shallow dish, combine panko crumbs, chili powder, paprika, 1 tablespoon minced garlic, and ½ teaspoon salt. Lightly beat egg in a second shallow dish. Dredge chicken in egg, then coat in crumbs.

4. Heat a thin layer of oil in a sauté pan over medium heat. When oil is hot, add chicken and cook for 3-4 minutes per side. Remove to a paper towel-lined plate. When cool enough to handle, cut chicken into thin evenly sized strips.

5. Prepare the red cabbage salad: In a small bowl, combine cabbage, vinegar, oil, sugar, and salt. Set aside.

6. Prepare the honey-garlic dipping sauce: In a small bowl, whisk together mayonnaise, water, honey, garlic, paprika, and pepper.

7. Assemble the wraps: Spread a tablespoon of the honey-garlic dipping sauce across the bottom-center of the wrap. Top with onions, chicken strips, and ¼ cup red cabbage. Make sure the filling is evenly distributed.

YIELD
30 roll-ups

You don't have to wait for a special occasion. Skip the skewers and serve these wraps as a complete weekday dinner. Put all the components on the table and let everyone roll their own sandwiches.

Keeping the wraps wrapped tightly in plastic wrap until ready to slice will keep them from unraveling. You can even slice right through the plastic.

WHENEVER I sit down to create a menu for a party I'm hosting, I think about how I can dress up my family's latest weeknight favorites. One of those favorites includes Leah's crispy chicken wraps, which she stuffs with onions, red cabbage, well-seasoned shnitzel, and an awesome sauce, because, as she believes, a good sandwich deserves layers. And I agree! This adapted version takes the dish from the dinette table to the dining room. —V.

AHEAD: Although best fresh, these skewers can be assembled earlier in the day. Serve at room temperature or reheat briefly so as not to cook the cabbage.

HONEY-GARLIC DIPPING SAUCE

½ cup	mayonnaise
¼ cup	water
2 Tbsp	honey
2	garlic cloves, crushed
¼ tsp	paprika
•	pinch coarse black pepper

Fold the bottom of the wrap over the filling and tuck under very tightly. Fold in the sides and continue to roll, egg roll-style, holding your fingers under the roll so that it remains very tight. Slice each wrap, sushi-style, into six pieces. Secure by threading a skewer through the edge of the wrap and the chicken. Repeat with remaining wraps and serve with remaining honey-garlic dipping sauce.

Silan Chicken Salad

INGREDIENTS

¼ cup	date honey (silan)
1 Tbsp	soy sauce
2	garlic cloves, crushed
1¼ lbs	boneless chicken breasts, cut into thin strips

SALAD

1	head Romaine lettuce, chopped
2 cups	shredded green cabbage
10-12	cherry tomatoes, halved
¼ cup	dried cranberries
3 Tbsp	peanuts

DRESSING

1½-2 Tbsp	date honey (silan)
2 Tbsp	vinegar
2-3 Tbsp	oil
1 Tbsp	sugar
1 tsp	salt
¼ tsp	coarse black pepper

INSTRUCTIONS

1. In a medium bowl, combine date honey, soy sauce, and garlic. Add chicken strips and marinate at room temperature for at least 30 minutes.

2. Spray a grill pan with nonstick cooking spray. Heat grill pan over medium-high heat. Remove chicken strips from marinade and grill until cooked through, 3-4 minutes per side. Remove chicken from pan. Thread each strip onto a skewer.

3. Prepare the dressing: In a small bowl, whisk together date honey, vinegar, oil, sugar, salt, and pepper.

4. In a large bowl, combine lettuce, cabbage, tomatoes, dried cranberries, and peanuts. Toss with dressing. To plate, top each individual serving of salad with 2 chicken skewers.

Make your own date honey! Quick way: Combine ½ cup pitted dates and ½ cup water. Microwave for 1 minute (or bring to a boil in a small saucepan), then blend well. Slow way: Combine the dates and water and refrigerate for 24 hours. The dates will dissolve on their own.

YIELD
6-7 servings

TIDBIT:
When the Torah lists the seven species native to the land of Israel, dvash, meaning "honey," refers to silan rather than to bee honey.

Use up your silan! Drizzle it over vanilla yogurt or ice cream or mix it with soy sauce and garlic and brush it over chicken before cooking.

SOME ingredients are common in one country, while almost nonexistent in others. Date honey is sold everywhere in Israel, while in the tri-state area, you need to go hunting. The last time I went through this effort to find an ingredient was when I discovered sweet chili sauce in 2008. In 2008, I made my own sweet chili sauce; then I realized that if there is a demand my supermarket would bring it in. Now every supermarket in a 10-mile radius carries sweet chili sauce (it's in the tangy Eggplant Salad on page 19).

Just as I did for sweet chili, I made my own silan. It's a lot simpler than making sweet chili sauce. See note for instructions. But I'm sure your grocer will have it on the shelves very soon.   –L.

AHEAD: Make the dressing and marinate your chicken in the refrigerator in advance. Then, grill the chicken and toss the salad together fresh.

Chestnut Chicken

INGREDIENTS

18	drumettes
¼ cup	oil
1	onion, diced
2	garlic cloves, crushed
1 tsp	chopped fresh ginger
¼ cup	soy sauce
¼ cup	red wine
2 Tbsp	sugar
½ tsp	salt
•	pinch coarse black pepper
¾ cup	roasted chestnuts

INSTRUCTIONS

1. Place chicken into a 9 x 13-inch baking pan.

2. Heat oil in a sauté pan over medium heat. Add onion and sauté until soft, 5-7 minutes. Add garlic and ginger and sauté an additional 1-2 minutes. Add in soy sauce, red wine, sugar, salt, and pepper. Stir to combine. Pour mixture over chicken. Marinate at room temperature for 30 minutes (refrigerate if you will marinate longer).

3. Cover and bake for 90 minutes for chicken bottoms or 45 minutes for chicken drumettes. Uncover, add chestnuts, and bake for an additional 20-30 minutes or until chicken is golden.

YIELD
4-6 servings

We used chestnuts that are already roasted and peeled and sold in a bag.

See how we styled this recipe in Plate It! on page 66.

ROASTED chestnuts are a winter comfort food. We roast them fresh and eat them hot, being careful not to burn our mouths. My family loves chestnuts, but whenever I wanted to make a recipe using them, it was so much work to roast and peel, only to use them as an ingredient. A couple of years ago, pre-roasted and peeled chestnuts came out on the market. Now, it's easy to use them in recipes and we can enjoy the flavor without all the work. When it comes to eating chestnuts plain, fresh hot chestnuts in the shell are still the best.   –L.

AHEAD: You can prepare the sauce ahead of time, or marinate the chicken earlier in the day and bake fresh. You can also freeze the raw chicken with the marinade.

PLATE IT!

Serve your Sea Bass with Sun-Dried Tomato Tapenade (page 98) just like we did.

1 You'll need a julienne peeler, zucchini, and a lemon or lime to complete this sea bass serving idea.

2 Julienne the zucchini and place it into a bowl.

3 Squeeze the citrus over the zucchini and let it sit for a few minutes. The acid in the citrus will "cook" the zucchini, making it limp.

4 Twirl the zucchini with a fork and place it in the center of your appetizer plate.

5 Top with a portion of fish.

6 Finish the dish with a mound of sun-dried tomato tapenade.

FISH

Crunchy Tempura Roll

INGREDIENTS

2 cups	sushi rice
3 Tbsp	rice vinegar
1½ tsp	salt, or to taste
7	nori sheets
4 oz	Tofutti cream cheese (from 8-oz container)
1	avocado, cut into strips
4 oz	sugar snap peas
4 oz	Nova salmon, cut into thin strips
•	oil for frying
•	dipping sauces (see notes)

TEMPURA COATING

1 cup	flour
1 cup	water
1	egg
2½ cups	panko crumbs

INSTRUCTIONS

1. Prepare rice according to package directions. Stir rice vinegar and salt into rice and let cool.

2. Place a sheet of nori, shiny side down, onto a bamboo mat. Using a wooden spoon or paddle, pat rice over half of the nori sheet. Spread cream cheese down the center of the rice, followed by layers of avocado, sugar snap peas, and salmon.

3. Using the mat, roll the edge of the nori over the filling and continue to roll and shape the sushi into a tight cylinder. Fill and roll the remaining nori sheets.

4. Prepare the tempura coating: In a shallow bowl, combine flour, water, and egg. Whisk to combine. Place panko crumbs into a second shallow dish.

5. Slice the sushi rolls in halves or thirds. Coat all sides in the batter, and then in panko crumbs.

6. Heat 1 to 1½ inches oil in a small saucepan. Fry sushi until panko is golden brown, about 30 seconds on each side. Remove to a paper towel-lined plate. Slice using a sharp serrated knife and serve with Spicy Mayo and Sweet Teriyaki Sauce (see notes).

YIELD
7 jumbo rolls

Don't leave out the dipping sauces! For Spicy Mayo, combine 4 heaping tablespoons mayonnaise, 1½ teaspoons sriracha chili sauce, 1 teaspoon lemon juice, and a dash of soy sauce.

The second sauce on this plate is sweet teriyaki dipping sauce. We used the same sauce in step 2 of the Teriyaki Mushrooms on page 26.

IF I had to pick only one restaurant-style dish to enjoy on a desert island, it would be fried sushi. When I make it for dinner with the dipping sauces, I don't have to bother preparing anything else (my kids like it with nothing inside). I've also served it as an appetizer for a fish course when I had to feed 80 and didn't want to spend a ton of money. For this dish, the effort is worth it.

–V.

AHEAD: You can prepare these rolls earlier in the day and fry fresh. The dipping sauces can be prepared in advance and refrigerated.

Salmon with a Pocket

INGREDIENTS

4	(4-6 oz) salmon fillets
½ cup	lemon juice
1	red pepper, cut into thin strips
2	Portobello mushroom caps, sliced
3-4	garlic cloves, crushed
1 tsp	salt
½ tsp	coarse black pepper
3-4 Tbsp	olive oil

INSTRUCTIONS

1. Preheat oven to 375ºF.

2. In a shallow dish, marinate salmon in lemon juice for 15 minutes. Rinse.

3. Slit the belly of each salmon fillet horizontally through the middle, creating an opening. Stuff with pepper and mushroom slices and trim the vegetables even with the edge of the fillet. Place fillets into a 9 x 13-inch baking pan.

4. Season fillets with garlic, salt, and pepper. Drizzle with olive oil. Cover and bake for 15 minutes. Uncover and bake until fish flakes easily with a fork, 5-7 minutes. Serve hot or at room temperature.

YIELD
4-6 servings

INSPIRED BY
COOKKOSHER MEMBER
rabash

Does your garlic sometimes look green? Garlic turns green either when it's not fresh or when it has come into contact with acid.

You can swap out the mushrooms and peppers for other veggies. Green beans and carrots work well, too.

WHEN we speak to chefs, their mantra is always, "Start with high quality ingredients, and go with what's in season and fresh. When you have good ingredients, good dishes are simple." This recipe is a great example.

Fresh salmon doesn't need much to make it taste good and this dish highlights its flavors.   –L.

AHEAD: You can prep this earlier in the day: Keep refrigerated, and bake when you're ready to serve.

Seed-Crusted Salmon

INGREDIENTS

4	(4-6 oz) salmon fillets
3 Tbsp	honey
1 Tbsp	soy sauce
¼ cup	salted sunflower seeds
¼ cup	chopped pecans
¼ cup	raw pumpkin seeds (pepitas)
2 Tbsp	sesame seeds
1 Tbsp	poppy seeds
1 Tbsp	minced garlic

INSTRUCTIONS

1. Preheat oven to 350°F. Line a baking pan with parchment paper. Place fish into prepared pan.

2. In a small bowl, combine honey and soy sauce. Smear over tops and sides of salmon.

3. In a small bowl, combine sunflower seeds, pecans, pumpkin seeds, sesame seeds, poppy seeds, and garlic. Press topping onto fish. Bake for 20-25 minutes.

YIELD
4 servings

You can also add flax seeds to the seed mixture.

Mix additional honey and soy sauce and use it to drizzle the plate when serving.

LOTS of people love a fish with a nut crust. But seeds are often neglected in favor of pistachios, pecans, and almonds. This time, we give seeds their due in a salmon dish that's very wholesome and gourmet-tasting.
–L.

AHEAD: Though you can make your nut mix in advance and coat your fish earlier in the day, the fish should be baked fresh.

Sea Bass WITH Sun-Dried Tomato Tapenade

INGREDIENTS

1½ lbs	sea bass fillets
¼ tsp	salt
•	pinch coarse black pepper
¼ cup	mayonnaise
1½ tsp	sriracha sauce
1 tsp	lemon juice
1 tsp	honey
¾ cup	panko crumbs
3	garlic cloves, minced
1 tsp	dried parsley

SUN-DRIED TOMATO TAPENADE

½ cup	sun-dried tomatoes
2 tsp	fresh minced basil
2	garlic cloves
½ tsp	salt
2 Tbsp	olive oil
½ Tbsp	balsamic vinegar

INSTRUCTIONS

1. Preheat oven to 350°F. Cut fillets into 2½-3-inch squares. Place fillets into a baking pan and season with salt and pepper.

2. In a small bowl, combine mayonnaise, sriracha sauce, lemon juice, and honey. Spread mayonnaise mixture over top and sides of the sea bass.

3. In a second small bowl, combine panko crumbs, garlic, and parsley. Press onto top and sides of the sea bass. Bake for 20 minutes or until fish flakes easily with a fork. To give the crumbs a nice golden color, broil on a middle oven rack for an additional 1 to 2 minutes.

4. Prepare the tapenade: Soak sun-dried tomatoes in boiling water for 15 minutes. Drain well.

5. In the bowl of a mini chopper or food processor, combine sun-dried tomatoes, basil, garlic, salt, olive oil, and balsamic vinegar. Pulse to combine.

Even those who don't like spicy foods will enjoy how a teensy bit of sriracha complements mild sea bass. Want more heat? Add ½ teaspoon sriracha to the tapenade, too.

YIELD
4-6 servings

TIDBIT:
It takes 14 pounds of tomatoes to produce 1 pound of sun-dried tomatoes. That 93 percent volume loss is all water.

How did we prepare the extras you see on this plate? See Plate It! on page 90.

OFTEN when Leah or I attend a wedding, we send each other photos of the food we're eating. One night at 10:11 p.m., I received a photo of a sea bass appetizer on my phone. —V.

My cousin sitting next to me asked if I could figure out the recipe for the sea bass that was in front of us. I took a photo and sent it to Victoria with the following message: "Sea bass. Honey very little. Mayo. Chili sauce ... a drop to make it look orange. Seasoned panko crumbs."   —L.

I got the hint. The next night, I enjoyed perhaps my favorite version of sea bass yet. Thanks to Leah's cousin for asking!   —V.

AHEAD: Though sea bass must be baked fresh, you can bread it up to one day in advance and keep covered in the refrigerator until ready to bake. Store the tapenade, refrigerated in an airtight container, for up to 1 month.

Seared Pepper Tuna WITH Gemelli Salad

INGREDIENTS

4	(4-oz) sushi-grade tuna steaks
1 Tbsp	soy sauce
1½ tsp	Montreal steak seasoning
1 tsp	minced onion
1 Tbsp	oil

SALAD

12 oz	spring greens
2	carrots, shredded
1	beet, shredded
1 cup	cooked gemelli pasta
1 Tbsp	sesame seeds
¼ cup	slivered toasted almonds

DRESSING

2 Tbsp	oil
2 Tbsp	soy sauce
2 Tbsp	rice vinegar
½ tsp	sugar
½ tsp	salt
•	pinch coarse black pepper

INSTRUCTIONS

1. Rub soy sauce onto each side of the tuna steaks and season generously with Montreal steak seasoning and minced onion.

2. Heat oil in a sauté pan over medium-high heat. When oil is hot, add tuna (it should sizzle) and cook for 1-2 minutes per side. The tuna should still be pink in the middle.

3. Prepare the salad: In a large bowl, combine lettuce, carrots, beet, pasta, sesame seeds, and almonds.

4. Prepare the dressing: In a small bowl, combine oil, soy sauce, rice vinegar, sugar, salt, and pepper. Toss dressing with salad and serve alongside tuna steaks.

YIELD
4 servings

Raw beets add great color and crunch to a salad, and, unlike cooked beets, the color won't bleed and turn everything red. When it comes to the greens, a head of Romaine lettuce or Napa cabbage will also work well in this salad.

The quality of your tuna really matters. Tuna that is not sushi-grade will not taste nearly as good.

FRESH sushi-grade tuna is my favorite type of fish. I once asked a crowd of 150 women at a food demonstration if anyone else loves tuna as much as I do. No one raised her hand. When I asked why, one person commented, "It's dry." Now, for all of you who think that tuna is dry, that's because you've only eaten it overcooked. At that same demonstration, I seared the tuna for only a minute or two on each side and left the inside pink (a MUST!). After fighting over all the samples, lots of women became tuna lovers that day.   –V.

AHEAD: Tuna must be seared fresh. The good news is that it only takes a couple of minutes!

Tangy Tilapia Nuggets

INGREDIENTS

1 lb	tilapia fillets, cut into nuggets
1-2	eggs
¾ cup	bread crumbs
5 Tbsp	oil, divided

TANGY SAUCE

½ cup	apricot jam
½ cup	ketchup
½ cup	teriyaki sauce
2 tsp	garlic powder
1 Tbsp	vinegar

INSTRUCTIONS

1. Preheat oven to 350°F.

2. Lightly beat eggs in a shallow dish. Place bread crumbs into a second shallow dish.

3. Dip nuggets into eggs, then coat with bread crumbs.

4. Heat half the oil in a sauté pan over medium heat. When hot, add nuggets in batches and fry until bread crumbs are toasted, about 2 minutes per side. The fish does not need to be further cooked at this point. Place nuggets into a baking pan.

5. Prepare the sauce: In a small bowl, combine apricot jam, ketchup, teriyaki sauce, garlic powder, and vinegar. Pour over tilapia nuggets. Bake for 15 to 20 minutes (the sauce should appear to have thickened).

YIELD
24-30 nuggets

INSPIRED BY
COOKKOSHER MEMBER
doctor

TIDBIT:
In modern Hebrew, tilapia is called "amnun." It takes it name from eim, meaning "mother," and nun, Aramaic for "fish." This is because newborn tilapias live in their mothers' mouths for protection.

You can also serve the nuggets plain and use the tangy sauce as a dip. Fry the nuggets until cooked through. You'll need only half the sauce.

GROWING up, my mother would fry flounder as a way to convince us to eat fish. She'd tell us it was a pareve version of our favorite food: shnitzel. Today, if you want adults (and kids!) to enjoy fish, try this recipe. These sweet and tangy nuggets are the perfect appetizer for non-fish lovers. As a last resort, tell them it's a pareve version of their favorite food: chicken nuggets (with a dip). -L.

AHEAD: These tangy nuggets will freeze well, before or after baking.

PLATE IT!

Your guests will love having their personal portion of Parmesan Sticks with Creamy Marinara Dipping Sauce (page 114). Here's how we serve it.

1 You'll need a rimless wine glass.

2 Carefully spoon some of the Creamy Marinara Dipping Sauce into the bottom of the glass. Be careful not to drip any on the sides.

3 Fill one side of the glass with eggplant, asparagus, or avocado sticks, or a combination of them all.

4 To have the fork stand, pierce one of the sticks with it.

DAIRY

Cheesy Onion Rolls

INGREDIENTS

2 cups	flour
1 tsp	salt
1 tsp	sugar
½ tsp	active dry yeast
1 Tbsp	butter
1 cup	water

FILLING

3 Tbsp	butter, melted
1	onion, diced
½ cup	mozzarella cheese
1	egg, lightly beaten

INSTRUCTIONS

1. In the bowl of an electric mixer, combine flour, salt, sugar, yeast, butter, and water. Knead until dough is smooth. Remove to a greased bowl. Cover with a clean dish towel and let rise for 1 hour.

2. Prepare the filling: Combine butter and onions.

3. Divide dough into 8 balls. Flatten each ball into a circle or square. Place a spoonful onion mixture and 2 spoons cheese in the center and fold two ends over the filling. Place an additional spoon onion mixture on top and fold over two remaining ends.

4. Brush with beaten egg and bake for 25 minutes.

YIELD
8 rolls

TIDBIT:
The Hebrew word for cheese, "gevinah," appears only once in the Tanach, in the Book of Job (10:10).

If you're in a rush, you can use store-bought pizza dough.

THE topic of our next cookbook should be 60+ recipes you can make using pizza dough! Now all I need to do is convince Victoria. This time, pizza dough is repurposed in a buttery onion roll. We thought: If we're serving bread at the start of a dairy meal, there's no sense in keeping it plain and pareve. If you ever find these, warm in a restaurant's bread basket, we don't know if you'll still have room for the meal.   —L.

AHEAD: These rolls will freeze nicely. Cover and rewarm when ready to serve.

Avocado Cigars

INGREDIENTS

1	ripe avocado
4	garlic cloves, crushed
1	plum tomato, seeds removed, finely diced
2 tsp	lemon juice
1 tsp	olive oil
¼ tsp	salt or to taste
•	pinch coarse black pepper
6-8	(6-inch) wheat tortillas
½ cup	shredded cheese
¼ tsp	chili powder
¼ tsp	paprika

INSTRUCTIONS

1. Preheat oven to 350°F. Line a baking sheet with parchment paper.

2. In a medium bowl, mash avocado. Add garlic, tomato, lemon juice, olive oil, salt, and pepper.

3. Spread 1 tablespoon of the mixture across the bottom-center of each wrap. Top with 1 tablespoon cheese. Fold the bottom of the wrap up over the filling. Fold in sides and roll up, jelly-roll style. Secure with a toothpick.

4. Place cigars on prepared baking sheet. Spray tops of cigars with nonstick cooking spray and sprinkle with chili powder and paprika. Bake for 8-10 minutes, or until lightly browned. Remove toothpick after baking.

YIELD
6-8 cigars

Want to prevent your tomato salad from getting mushy? How about preventing your sandwich with its slice of tomato from getting soggy? The trick is to use plum tomatoes, removing the seeds.

I showed this recipe at a few food demonstrations this year. It's not because I think it's the most unusual dish, and not because it's so complicated that you need live in-person instructions to prepare it. I've chosen this one because it's one of the quickest appetizers to prepare. Some people need to see it to believe how fast they come together (and how delicious they taste ... for those who got to sample). As they say, seeing is believing.   —L

AHEAD: The cigars can be prepared earlier in the day and served at room temperature.

Tomato Tart

INGREDIENTS

½ lb	puff pastry dough, defrosted
½ cup	mayonnaise
½ cup	sour cream
½ Tbsp	dried oregano or basil
½ tsp	salt
½ tsp	pepper
3	tomatoes, sliced

INSTRUCTIONS

1. Preheat oven to 350°F. Line a baking sheet with parchment paper.

2. Roll out puff pastry dough to ¼-inch thick. Using a knife, mark a 1-inch border around the edges of the dough without cutting all the way through.

3. Place dough on baking sheet and bake for 10-15 minutes, until dough is just beginning to puff up.

4. Combine mayonnaise, sour cream, oregano, salt, and pepper and spread over the dough, staying within the border. Layer sliced tomatoes on top.

5. Bake an additional 40 minutes, or until tart is golden. Serve at room temperature.

YIELD
8 servings

INSPIRED BY
COOKKOSHER MEMBER
cook 7

If they're available, use heirloom tomatoes and layer in strips of different colors.

ONE Friday afternoon last summer, I spoke to my friend Krassie, who told me she was preparing a tomato tart. I thought a tomato tart was that great "something" that could give a dairy meal some color and pizzazz and told her, "One day I need to get that recipe from you."

This recipe is an easy way to take advantage of sweet summer tomatoes. I also love that it uses pantry staples and turns them into something beautiful.   –L.

AHEAD: This tart will freeze well, before or after baking.

Sweet Potato and Leek Quiche

INGREDIENTS

2	ready-to-bake pie shells
¼ cup	(½ stick) butter
1	red onion, diced
1	onion, diced
1	leek, diced
2	medium sweet potatoes, finely diced
¼ cup	flour
⅔ cup	milk
1¼ cup	heavy cream
1 tsp	salt
•	pinch coarse black pepper
4	eggs, lightly beaten
½ cup	shredded cheese

INSTRUCTIONS

1. Preheat oven to 300°F. Prick bottom of pie shells with a fork. Bake for 10 minutes. Remove from oven. Raise oven temperature to 350°F.

2. Melt butter in a large sauté pan over medium heat. Add onions and leek and sauté until completely soft, 20-25 minutes.

3. Meanwhile, place sweet potatoes in a microwave-safe dish. Add water to cover the bottom of the dish. Microwave for 6 minutes. Drain.

4. Add sweet potatoes to the onions and sauté for an additional 2-3 minutes. Remove from heat and stir in flour, milk, cream, salt, and pepper. Let cool. Stir in eggs. Pour into prepared pie shells. Top with cheese. Bake for 45 minutes to 1 hour.

YIELD
2 pies

INSPIRED BY
COOKKOSHER MEMBER
cookmama

It doesn't take less time to make one pie instead of two, so bake it and keep it in the freezer for an easy addition to a dinner or a brunch.

I think that we're tired of making and eating quiches from mushrooms, broccoli, or spinach. This quiche, though, is one that gets me excited to slice up and enjoy. Add a salad and some coffee and invite the girls over for brunch.
–L.

AHEAD: The quiches will freeze well. Let thaw and reheat before serving, being careful not to allow the crust to burn.

Parmesan Sticks WITH Creamy Marinara Dipping Sauce

INGREDIENTS

2	eggs
½ cup	grated Parmesan cheese
½ cup	panko crumbs
½ tsp	dried basil
½ tsp	dried oregano
1 lb	asparagus, tops, bottoms, and leaves trimmed OR 3 ripe but firm avocados, sliced into strips OR ½ eggplant, cut into sticks OR a combination

CREAMY MARINARA DIPPING SAUCE

¼ cup	marinara sauce
2 Tbsp	mayonnaise
1	garlic clove, crushed
⅛ tsp	chili powder

INSTRUCTIONS

1. Preheat oven to 425°F. Line a baking sheet with parchment paper.

2. Lightly beat eggs in a wide shallow bowl. Combine Parmesan cheese, panko crumbs, basil, and oregano into a second shallow bowl.

3. Dredge vegetable sticks, a few at a time, in egg. Let the excess egg drip off and place the vegetable sticks onto the Parmesan/panko mixture. Using a spoon, spoon some of the Parmesan/panko mixture over the vegetable sticks to cover the top and sides. (Do not place eggy fingers into the Parmesan/panko crumb mixture when coating the sticks or the egg will cause it to clump).

4. Place sticks on the prepared baking sheet. Bake for 12 minutes, or until golden.

5. Prepare dipping sauce: In a small bowl, whisk together marinara sauce, mayonnaise, garlic, and chili powder. Serve with Parmesan Sticks.

> You can also prepare this recipe using zucchini, sweet potato, or butternut squash sticks, but they'll take much longer to bake.

YIELD
36 sticks

TIDBIT:
Authentic Parmesan cheese (parmigiano reggiano) is produced with the help of calf rennet. It can still be made kosher since the rennet only acts as the catalyst for the cheese to form. Proper rabbinic supervision is required.

See Plate It! on page 104 for tips on serving this dish.

AT a dairy meal, I'm always searching for the veggie side dish on menus that are usually a carb fest. But I don't want another string bean or roasted veggie when there is cheese around. These fill that craving for something between light and indulgent.

And they're baked! That's good because 1) there's no standing over a hot frying pan and 2) you won't feel so bad when you've polished off the whole tray and need to make a new batch for your company. –V.

AHEAD: You can bake these earlier in the day and serve at room temperature. Or, coat them in crumbs up to a day ahead and bake fresh so that they're hot.

PLATE IT!

Want to make a beautiful braid to enclose your Apple Cherry Strudel (page 118)? Here's how we do it.

1 The recipe will make 2 strudels, so begin by rolling out half of your dough on a Silpat or parchment paper.

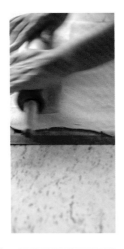

2 Use a ruler to help you cut off the uneven edges.

3 Use the same ruler as a border as you slice diagonal slits along each side of the dough.

4 Sprinkle the center of the dough with bread crumbs; then add the apple and cherry filling.

5 Fold the top two triangles over the edge of the filling. You can use the dough on the other side to cover the opposite end of the strudel as well.

6 Braid your strudel by folding each strip over the filling on the diagonal, alternating sides.

SWEET

Apple Cherry Strudel

INGREDIENTS

2 cups	flour
1	egg yolk
6 Tbsp	water
1 cup	margarine, at room temperature
4-5	Cortland apples, grated
2 Tbsp	plus 1 tsp sugar, divided
2 tsp	vanilla sugar
1½ cups	(6 oz) frozen pitted cherries
1 tsp	flour
3-4 Tbsp	breadcrumbs
•	confectioners' sugar, for dusting

INSTRUCTIONS

1. Preheat oven to 350°F.

1. In a large bowl, combine flour, egg yolk, water, and margarine. Using your hands, knead together until dough forms. Set aside.

2. In a large bowl, combine apples, 2 tablespoons sugar, and vanilla sugar. In a small bowl, combine cherries, 1 teaspoon sugar, and flour.

3. Divide dough in half. Roll out each half on floured parchment paper to a 10 x 12-inch rectangle. Sprinkle breadcrumbs vertically down the centers. Top breadcrumbs with apples, then cherries. Cut ½-inch diagonal slits next to the filling along the sides of the dough (see Plate It! on page 116). Fold slits over the dough, alternating sides, to cover the filling.

4. Transfer strudels on the parchment paper to a baking sheet. Bake until lightly golden, about 40-50 minutes. Dust generously with confectioners' sugar.

> For an easy strudel, simply roll and fill dough; then fold sides over the filling and cut a few slits through the top. Bake as instructed.

YIELD
2 loaves

TIDBIT:
The Hebrew term for the @ sign used in e-mails is shtrudel, due to its resemblance to the cross-section cut of the pastry of the same name.

VICTORIA and I get along really well. That's until we discuss sweet side dishes. At every meal, I always need a sweet side dish: apple crisp, plum pie …. Victoria is always shocked that I consider those side dishes. She'll eat them for dessert.

We might not agree when sweet dishes should be served. (I don't yet forgive her for serving my babka for dessert on a Friday night … that was supposed to be for breakfast!), but we agreed to disagree.

Victoria still claims this recipe is dessert, but she also thinks that including sweet side dishes is a fabulous excuse to have a dessert chapter in a side dish cookbook.

–L.

AHEAD: The strudels freeze very well. Freeze after braiding and bake fresh.

Peach Cracker Crumble

INGREDIENTS

2 Tbsp	honey
2 lbs	peaches, sliced
•	juice of ½ lemon
2 cups	blueberries
1 Tbsp	flour

CRACKER CRUMBLE

1½ cups	crushed saltines (not unsalted)
¾ cup	brown sugar
5 Tbsp	oil
½ tsp	cinnamon

INSTRUCTIONS

1. Preheat oven to 350°F. In a small microwave-safe dish, microwave honey for 20 seconds. In a large bowl, toss honey, peaches, and lemon juice. Pour peaches into a deep 9-inch baking dish or individual ramekins.

2. Prepare the crumble: In a large bowl, combine saltines, brown sugar, oil, and cinnamon. Mix ⅓ of the crumble mixture with the peaches. Bake for 20 minutes.

3. Raise oven temperature to 400°F. In a medium bowl, toss blueberries with flour. Layer blueberries over cooked peaches. Top with remaining crumble, packing it in to form a crust. Bake until golden and crisp, about 15 minutes.

In the wintertime, you can substitute apples and pears for the peaches and blueberries. You'll need to add 10-15 minutes to the first baking time. Frozen peaches and frozen blueberries will also work.

YIELD
10-12 servings

TIDBIT:
The word "peach," as well as its official scientific name, persica (and its Hebrew name, afarsec) derives from the belief that peaches came from Persia. We now know that the fruit originated in China.

We served these crumbles in mini Mason jars.

THE only problem with this dish is that whenever I bring it to my mom for Shabbat, half of it is always missing.

When it came time to bring it to my mother-in-law, though, I tried very hard to make sure that I would be bringing it complete and wouldn't let any spoons enter. That Friday, I packed up the car, complete with clothing, kids, and crumble, and then patiently waited for my husband to arrive so we could leave. All the while, the warm crumble sat on my lap, teasing me with its cinnamon aroma. It's a good thing I hadn't packed any spoons.   –V.

AHEAD: This crumble will freeze very well. If freezing before baking, let thaw and bake as directed in step 3. If freezing after baking, let thaw, cover, and reheat. Amount of time will vary based on the size of the dish used.

Mango AND Pineapple Salad WITH Citrus Sauce

INGREDIENTS

1	pineapple, finely diced
1	(16-oz) bag frozen strawberries, finely diced
2	mangos, finely diced
⅓ cup	sugar
1½ cups	orange juice
⅓ cup	lemon juice

INSTRUCTIONS

1. Place all the fruit into a large plastic container with a lid.

2. In a small saucepan over medium-high heat, combine sugar, orange juice, and lemon juice. Boil until sugar is dissolved, about 1 minute. Pour hot liquid over fruit. Cover and refrigerate until fruit is cool.

Add some seasonal fruit to the salad, like blueberries and cherries in the summer, and pomegranate and citrus in the winter.

YIELD
6 servings

TIDBIT:
Even though pineapple is considered a fruit, its blessing is ha'adamah, like that of a vegetable. This is because pineapples grow close to the ground in a bush.

EVERYONE loves a fruit salad, except the host, who doesn't want to be busy chopping fruit into neat dice on the day she's entertaining. Most fruit salads must be chopped fresh, or they'll get soggy. Not this one. Adding the tangy sauce preserves the fruit, even when marinating in the refrigerator for a few days. You can prepare this on Friday and serve it as a refreshing appetizer for *Seudah Shelishit*. Sometimes it just takes a simple technique to make all our lives a bit easier. —V.

AHEAD: This fruit salad can be prepared up to 3 days ahead. Keep refrigerated in an airtight container until ready to serve.

Whiskey Sweet Potatoes

INGREDIENTS

6	small sweet potatoes
½ tsp	coarse salt, or to taste
⅛ tsp	coarse black pepper

WHISKEY SAUCE

5 Tbsp	brown sugar
1 Tbsp	whiskey
1 Tbsp	honey
2 Tbsp	oil

INSTRUCTIONS

1. Preheat oven to 425°F. Place sweet potatoes on a baking tray. Bake for 20 minutes.

2. Slice sweet potatoes in half.

3. Meanwhile, prepare the whiskey sauce: In a small saucepan, combine brown sugar, whiskey, honey, and oil. Cook over medium heat until sugar is dissolved, 1-2 minutes. Brush sauce over cut sweet potatoes and season with salt and pepper.

4. Return sweet potatoes to the oven and bake, uncovered, for an additional 20 minutes.

YIELD
4-6 servings

You can also cut the sweet potatoes into wedges or rounds. Toss with some oil, salt, and pepper. Cover and bake for 1 hour. Uncover, toss with whiskey sauce, and bake an additional 20 minutes.

I always wondered why I never focused so much on the dessert course. Yes, I like dessert just as much as anyone else. But, possibly, I satisfy my sweet tooth with sweet side dishes. These have just the right amount of sweetness, while the whiskey gives the dish a flavor kick. Don't worry, you won't taste the alcohol.   –L.

AHEAD: Sweet potatoes are best prepared fresh, but you can prepare steps 1, 2, and 3 ahead of time and bake for the final time when ready to serve.

Make It a Main!

There's a reason why starters or appetizers are always the first chapter in a cookbook. It's not only because they're the first course of the meal! Usually, the prettiest and best recipes end up in the starters section because that's what readers see first. But that doesn't mean all those starters can't be a main course, whether you're entertaining or for a weeknight meal.

Coleslaw Balls with Jalapeno Dip *page 24*

Serve balls over spaghetti with your favorite tomato sauce or a tangy apricot sauce on page 102, for a vegetarian version of meatballs and spaghetti.

Winter Squash Ravioli *page 50*

Serve a full bowl of raviolis for a filling pasta meal.

Barbecue Noodles *page 52*

Add grilled chicken or fish to make a complete meal.

Crispy Beef *page 70*

Serve over rice for a complete meal.

Braised Steak Kebobs *page 72*

No adjustments are necessary — just increase portion size.

Lehme B'agine *page 74*

Roll out one large piece of pizza dough and top with the meat mixture for a meat pizza.

Falafel Cigars *page 76*

Double the quantity of filling ingredients and serve in a wrap or taco shell.

Veal-Stuffed Mushrooms *page 78*

Use the veal stuffing with larger Portobello mushrooms.

Shwarma Egg Rolls *page 82*

Serve the chicken filling in a pita with chummus or techineh.

Crispy Chicken Rolls *page 84*

Don't slice them! Simply serve the wraps whole.

Silan Chicken Salad *page 86*

Double the amount of chicken and marinade.

Chestnut Chicken *page 88*

Use chicken bottoms instead of drumettes and adjust cooking time. Bottoms will need 90 minutes covered and an additional 30 minutes uncovered.

Fish *pages 92-103*

All recipes in the fish chapter can be served as a main course. Simply adjust portion sizes.

Tomato Tart *page 110*

Add fresh mozzarella cheese to the top and enjoy it as a variation on pizza.

SOURCES

SET YOUR TABLE, Lakewood, NJ and Monsey, NY. 732.987.5569. Dishes, cutlery, tablecloths, and trays as featured on pages 29, 31, 41, 45, 53, 83, 95, 97, 99, 101, 107, 113, 115, 119, 123, and 125.

Mydrap cloth napkins and placemats, available in rolls of 12 in 7 sizes and over 30 colors and styles at *www.buymydrap.com*. Shown on pages 19, 25, 39, 59, 63, 69, 75, 97, 121.

NOIR SIGNATURE GIFTS. 732.363.3263. Serving platter, page 39.

CARMONA NEW YORK & CO. *www.carmonany.com*. Serving platter, page 79.

CB2. *www.cb2.com*. Trays, pages 19, 59, 93, 123. Dishes, pages 33, 57, 69, 71, 81, 109. Chopsticks, page 93.

THE FRITES SHOP. *www.fritesshop.com*. Paper French fry holders, pages 43 and 77.

IKEA. *www.ikea.com*. Tasting dishes, page 65.

THE CONTAINER STORE. *www.thecontainerstore.com*. Takeout containers, page 71.

PIER ONE IMPORTS. www.pierone.com. Trays, pages 57, 113, and 125. Tasting dishes, page 59. Sushi dish, page 93.